Guaranteed To Win!

A User Friendly Guide to Programming
Yourself for Success in Any Area of Your Life

By Barry Seedman, Ph.D.

T.C. Samson Publishing
New York, New York

FOREWARD

I met Barry Seedman, in March of 1995 when I enrolled in his Hypnotherapy Certification Weekend. This convinced me that my calling was truly in the field of Alternative Medicine.

Coming from a family of medical doctors, I set out in that direction and received my degree in Medicine from the University of Bologna, Italy. I began my professional career as a physician in Italy, but disillusionment with the limitations of traditional medicine led me to experiment with alternative healing modalities. In fact, it was my own use of self-hypnosis which led to a personal weight loss of 35 pounds, that convinced me of the merits of this Alternative Therapy.

When I returned to the United States, the one thing I knew was that I did not want to spend my career handing out medications. I considered other options, such as teaching and medical research and, when I enrolled in Barry's workshop, I was still searching. I had already completed training in Nutrition, Herbal Medicine, Oriental Medicine, and became a Reiki Master.

Then, a light in my head lit up! Because of my previous experience and success with self-hypnosis, I continued studying the mind and its presently known functions. This led me to further my studies in the art and science of

i

hypnosis. Barry's program certainly did impress me! It was comprehensive in that it dealt not only with induction of trance and direct suggestion, but also included many forms of therapy geared to client-hypnotherapist interaction. Barry showed us that by getting to the cause of the problem, whether it is mental, emotional, physical or spiritual, or any combination thereof, healing can truly take place. Once again, I was inspired to pursue my career in hypnosis and mind-body healing.

I followed through with advanced training in hypnotherapy, and have spent much time working with Barry in order to see a larger variety of clients and improve my techniques.

I continued to pursue the field of Mind-Body Medicine through the Clinical Training Program in Mind-Body Medicine offered at Harvard and The National Institute for the Clinical Applications of Behavioral Medicine. I have also become a Licensed Board Certified physician in Naturopathic Medicine. In fact, I recently opened my own center, The Hypnosis Healing Center in Clifton, NJ. Barry and I continue to consult with each other on special cases. Because of my medical training and insight, he invited me to sit on the Advisory Board of The Hypnosis Institute, which he directs.

I was delighted when he told me he was writing a book, and even more delighted when he ask me to preview it. In my opinion, Barry has written a succinct book in which, *through examples and anecdotes, he explains exactly how a person can reprogram him-or-herself for success in any area of life. I have read volumes of material about hypnosis, self-hypnosis and personal programming, and have found this to be one of the best "how to" books on the topic I have seen. Barry has taken his knowledge and put it in easy to read language and simple format so anyone, from an abstract artist to a zoologist, and any and every category in between, can use these techniques to achieve his or her own personal goals and objectives. I have seen this programming work with Barry's private clients and his students, with outstanding results.*

Using this book as a guide, you are "Guaranteed to Win."

Joseph A. Riccioli, M.D., Ph.D., N.D.
Director, The Hypnosis Healing Center
Clifton, NJ

For Nan, Mark, Rochelle, Lisa, Joe & Ryan

TABLE OF CONTENTS

INTRODUCTION

Very few people get to do, in life, what they really love --
Something they are truly good at.

You see, to me, the greatest thing you could ever do is show
another human being how to use his power, his energy, to
live the fullest life possible and to achieve his highest
potential - to teach another to empower himself.

I have worked and do work with many people who have
become heads of corporations, movie stars, and athletes
who have won Olympic medals and have broken world
records. I've shown others how to use the power of their
own minds to make fortunes, achieve excellence, overcome
medical and physical problems and disabilities, get rid of
addictions and unwanted habits, and create the life they
have always dreamed of.

For some years, I have been traveling all over the world
spreading the word about hypnosis. and how it can benefit
everyone. It's a simple process that is as easy as it is
effective. In one workshop, you can learn the techniques
to change your life forever. In one hypnotherapy session,
you can accomplish more than is possible with years and
years of traditional therapy.

In my workshops, I show people how to reduce stress,

change habits and behavior patterns easily and effortlessly, and I receive thousands of telephone calls and letters telling me how successful these methods are.

Now I am passing along this information to you. In this book you will learn how hypnosis works and how it can be used. To inspire you, I've included examples of astounding changes some of my personal clients have made. You will also be given simple exercises to learn self hypnosis. Finally, I will show you how to effectively program yourself to guarantee that you win at anything in life.

My avocation is truly my vocation. I really love my job! This is something that very few people can actually say. I have found a way to win at life, by enjoying each and every moment, and I want to share this with all of you.

I guarantee that you will succeed at each of your endeavors, just by following my simple self-programming steps.

CHAPTER 1 - HYPNOSIS 101

"Compared to what we ought to be, we are only half awake. We are making use of only a small portion of our physical and mental resources. Stating the thing broadly, the human individual thus lives far within his limits. He possesses power of various sorts that he habitually fails to use."

William James

Before you can begin to effectively use hypnosis, you must understand exactly what hypnosis is and how it works. I will, therefore, begin with a brief history and description of hypnosis, and why and how it works. Then you can begin to use the wonderful techniques on yourself.

What is Hypnosis?

There are many definitions for hypnosis. Generally, however, the common belief is that hypnosis is a relaxed state, resembling sleep, in which the subject's will is by-passed by the suggestion of the hypnotist. In otherwords, hypnosis would dominate or control the will by suggestion.

Hypnosis actually has little or nothing to do with passing through a relaxed state, nor does a person's "will" have anything to do with the process. Most simply put, hypnosis is a state of focused attention and heightened suggestibility.

It is a normal state of mind that we all go in and out of many times each day. For example, daydreaming is a form of hypnosis. While daydreaming, you are focused on a particular mental exercise, and have blocked off other stimuli around you. It is a state of focused attention.

Another example of hypnosis is something that has happened to most of us who drive a car. You are driving down the highway, your mind "off somewhere" and you drive past your exit. It's only two exits later that you realize what you have done. You were hypnotized! Your focused attention was on something else other than your driving.

Who was in control in both instances? You were, of course! In both of the above examples you were totally in control of your own mind. Think about it. In either case you would react should something endanger you. If you are daydreaming and someone shouts "fire," you would get up and run out of the room, reacting to the moment. While driving, even though focused on your own thoughts, you would have reacted had another car swerved toward you. In both cases, you were actually in control. Your attention was just focused elsewhere.

The term "hypnosis" has a real image problem. This image problem has stemmed from the media -- especially the movies --- where it is generally shown to be a technique used at the whim of some sinister character. The image problem actually began when this state was given its name.

The word "hypnosis," which means sleep in Greek, was actually mis-named by James Braid. Because he observed that the state appeared to look like sleep, he felt it appropriate. By the time it was discovered that sleep had nothing to do with this state, the term had already taken hold and stuck.

Movies have given hypnosis a particularly bad reputation. The hypnotist always seems to be taking total control of a weak person. The weak one is then sent out to do terrible things at the suggestion of the hypnotist. Again, this is all nonsense!

The person being hypnotized is always in control and will take suggestions only if he chooses to do so, and if they are not against his morals or ethics. If I were to hypnotize someone and suggest that the person go out and kill someone, would that suggestion work? No, unless that person is a killer. The average person, who knows right from wrong and has good morals and ethics, would not accept such a suggestion. In hypnosis, you are always in control and master of your own will.

I've now explained how hypnosis is a state of focused attention. It is also a state during which the subconscious mind is open to suggestion to create positive change.

How the mind works

In order to understand "heightened suggestibility," it is necessary to understand how the mind works.

The brain can be divided into two halves: The left brain, which is our analytical, critical, conscious mind; and the right brain, which is our creative, emotional, and subconscious mind. With hypnosis, we can bypass the left brain, or analytical part of the mind by putting it aside, usually through relaxation, and keeping it busy, to access the right brain, or subconscious. It is this side that must open up to suggestion in order to make permanent change.

Our brain can be compared to a computer. It is continuously being programmed and reprogrammed as we grow mentally and emotionally. As children, growing up from infancy to about 10 years of age, both our conscious and subconscious minds are open and working together to learn. At about age 10, the subconscious mind closes off, as our critical mind takes conscious precedence over our actions. In other words, behavioral programming becomes more difficult because we must re-access the subconscious mind to make permanent behavior change.

There are two ways to quickly access the subconscious mind: 1) through the emotions, and 2) through hypnosis. What we must remember as we access this part of our mind, is that this part closed down at about age 10, and this emotional, subconscious mind remains that 10-year-old emotional mind for the remainder of our lives. Therefore, when dealing with this part of our mind, we must talk with it and program it in language that a 10-year-old would understand.

There are a few other things about this portion of the mind we must know. First, the subconscious mind does not understand a joke. When the emotions open access to the subconscious mind, and something is said in a flippant or joking way, the subconscious mind will accept that statement as truth. As an example, consider a husband and wife having an argument. Emotions are high and the subconscious mind is wide open for programming access. The wife yells at her husband, "One day I'm going to kill you!" These may be words said in the heat of the moment, but they are now firmly implanted in the husband's subconscious mind, and the relationship between these two people may never be the same again.

Second, the subconscious mind does not understand or accept negatives. For example, if you tell your children not to put their feet on the couch, what's the first thing they do. They put their feet on the couch. Or, if I tell you not to think of a pink elephant, what's the first thing that comes to your mind? A pink elephant! Or, think about the phrase "Don't drink and drive!" The first thing that comes to mind is drinking while driving. This is why advertising around this problem is being changed to "Drive Sober!" A very positive statement.

Third, the subconscious mind does not understand the word "pretend." The 10 year old emotional mind that we spoke of earlier accepts the information as truth. Although this may seem difficult to accept, it's really true. Consider the old song "Put on a Happy Face." If, when we are unhappy or depressed about something, we pretend we're happy and we act happy, all of a sudden, without even realizing it, change takes place and those unhappy and depressed feelings have left us.

As children, pretending was really easy and simple for us. Our imaginations could take us far and away from reality. Pretending gave us confidence that we could do anything and be anything. By regaining the ability to pretend therefore, our self-confidence and self-esteem can be raised. We can tap into our wonderful imagination, and this allows us to expand ourselves beyond set limitations.

What all very successful people have in common is they do not feel limited, and they are not afraid to dream (or pretend). More about pretending later.

Accessing the Subconscious Mind for Permanent Change

We briefly talked about the two ways we can access the

subconscious mind: through the emotions and through hypnosis. But, why must we get to the subconscious mind to make permanent changes in our lives?

The subconscious mind holds all of our deep seated emotions. It's where painful and pleasurable lessons are filed. Let's face it, our emotions are part of everything we say and do. When we are consciously confronted with specific situations, it is our emotional mind which digs back into those files, seeking similar situations and the emotions connected with them. It is for this reason that, even though we consciously know we should react one way, we find ourselves doing just what we know we shouldn't. For example, how many times have you told yourself you would not loose your temper in a given situation, only to find yourself yelling and screaming and reverting to your same old ways the next time that situation occurs. The emotions take over.

In these situations it is our past programming that needs adjusting, and the only way to do this is to access the subconscious mind.

How is the State of Hypnosis Reached and the Subconscious Accessed?

Although hypnosis is a natural state of consciousness we go in and out of many times each day, there are also ways in which we can deliberately induce it. The hypnotist, for example, uses several different techniques, usually including some form of guided relaxation, to allow the conscious mind to be put aside or become dormant, in order that the subconscious mind can be opened for reprogramming.

Self-Hypnosis

We can also access our own subconscious mind through self-hypnosis. Most of us understand the concept of meditation. It is an exercise to relax ourselves and clear our minds by focusing on a mantra (a significant word, group of words, or sound) such as "Om" or "I am that I am." The key here is that we are emptying our mind of all thought. We do this to access our true feelings, to deal with problems or reduce the stress in our lives. In self-hypnosis, we access that same meditative, quieted, relaxed state. But, once there we give ourselves positive suggestion for changes we wish to make or goals we wish to reach. In other words, meditation is *listening* to ourselves by clearing our minds, while self-hypnosis is *talking* to ourselves by programming our minds.

For those of you who do not meditate, the easiest way to learn self-hypnosis is to have a private session with a hypnotherapist, and have the technique programmed into the subconscious. It is also possible to learn self-hypnosis on your own. Here is a simple exercise for you to do:

Sit back in a comfortable chair, with your feet flat on the floor and your arms at your side. Then, close your eyes, and take a deep breath. As you exhale just allow yourself to relax and begin to focus on the sentence, "I feel terrific!" Just mentally repeat this sentence to yourself, as you begin to imagine yourself feeling absolutely terrific. Imagine what you would look like and feel like when you think of yourself as "absolutely terrific." Just allow these images to run through your mind over and over and over for a few minutes. When you open your eyes, notice the change in how you feel.

If this simple exercise has made you notice even the slightest change in how you were originally feeling, then you have already begun to experience self-hypnosis. For some of you, this exercise will have made no difference. Here's where *pretending* comes into play. Just *pretend* you feel terrific. By pretending as you do this exercise day after day, all of a sudden, you will feel terrific. Then, by taking time each day to focus on a specific positive change, you will be on the road to winning!

Hypnosis vs. Hypnotherapy

Now that you have an idea of what hypnosis is, we can look at the term "hypnotherapy." Formed by the two words hypnosis (from the Greek "hypnos" meaning sleep) and therapy (also from Greek "therapeia," meaning "curative or healing"), it could therefore be defined as healing sleep or healing through hypnosis. Let's take this one step further and look at the term "heal," which actually is to make one whole or sound, or to free from anything bad such as illness or injury.

Hypnotherapy can therefore be said to be a technique which accesses the subconscious mind in order to make a person whole or sound, or to free that person from a bad habit or behavior.

Because hypnotherapy accesses the subconscious mind in order that permanent change can be made, it can do in a very short period of time (usually one session) what traditional psychotherapy may take years to accomplish. In my private practice I have seen incredible changes take place in just one session. Throughout the remainder of this book, you will learn about some of these, and how you can benefit from these techniques.

Reinforcement of Suggestion

No two people will respond to hypnosis in exactly the same way. While one person may feel "heaviness" another may feel "lightness." It is a very individual experience. Also, when a suggestion is made to one person, it may last the rest of his life, while for another person the suggestion may only last a few hours. It is for this reason that reinforcement of suggestion is necessary.

I always give my clients an audiotape, made during their session, to take home with them. I make this tape by including some relaxation, their goals and objectives, and their positive affirmations. As part of the contract for success between me and the client, I insist they listen to the tape once a day for at least 21 days.   The concept of 21 days comes from an old wives tale which claims that it "takes 21 days to make a habit and 21 days to break a habit." What 21 days of listening to reinforcement does is get the message to the subconscious mind that the conscious mind means business.

An example of the necessity of reinforcement can be illustrated by the case of a stockbroker who came to me for help with success and self-confidence. Cold calling phone solicitations were a major part of his job, and he found it extremely difficult to overcome refusals.   During our session, I had him imagine himself making his calls, easily and effortlessly talking with people, easily overcoming any objections and enjoying each call. I even had him enjoy the call if the prospect did say no. In fact, I suggested that he would feel even more excited about the next call if this happened. His imagery was good and the session went quite well. I then gave him his reinforcement tape and had him agree to listen to it once a day for the next 21 days.

He went to work at 9:00 AM the next day. At 9:15 AM he called me and said, "It's not working!" I told him to relax, that each person is different, but by listening to his tape each day, it would begin to work. At noon he called again and said "It's not working!" He called twice more that day to say "It's not working!" Each time, I explained he had to give it a chance. The next day he called me twice with the same statement. Then an amazing thing happened, late in the afternoon of the third day, he called one more time and said, "It's WORKING!"

It does work!

CHAPTER 2 - VISUALIZATION

Many different modalities talk about visualizing. In many guided meditations you are asked to "visualize" a scene, or to "visualize" an action. I know! I know! When you close your eyes, all you see is "black." I can't tell you how many times over the years clients and students have told me, "I just can't visualize. I just can't *see* what you're telling me to see." This is precisely why I am devoting a chapter to this concept.

In order to achieve your goals, whether it's to get that promotion, win that game, lose some weight, stop smoking, exercise more, work harder, be more creative, etc., you must be able to *see* yourself as having already achieved that goal. What I mean here by *see yourself*, does not necessarily mean closing your eyes and having a full color snapshot or motion picture appear. Some people have absolutely no trouble closing their eyes and having that full color image appear. Most, do. However, you can still visualize. What if we change the word from "visualize" to "imagine?" Maybe that would make it easier.

Visualization is really not so much **seeing**, as it is **knowing**. If I asked you to describe a golf ball, you would probably tell me that it's a little white ball with small indentations all over the surface. If you could not visualize, you could not tell me what it looked like. You see, it really is an accessing of knowledge that already exists in our mental files. All we are doing is retrieving that information.

Without visualization, without imagination, without previous experience, you could not describe the room you are in with your eyes closed. Granted, some of us have a bit more difficulty, but we can all do this. So, the next time you hear the word "visualize" and you close your eyes and see "black," just allow your mind go beyond or behind the "black" and retrieve that filed away knowledge that will allow you to **see**.

As an exercise, I would like you to do exactly what I suggested above. Just close your eyes for a moment and describe your immediate surroundings. If you are sitting, "see" the chair or seat; if you are lying down, "see" the bed, sofa, or lounge." Then "see" what's on your right; on your left; in front of you. Describe it.

Next, think about the last vacation you had. Where did you go? Close your eyes and describe where you stayed, what you saw and did there.

You see (no pun intended), you can visualize!

CHAPTER 3 - EFFECTING CHANGE THROUGH HYPNOSIS

In order for hypnotherapy to be effective, two things are necessary:

1. The client must accept the suggestions of the hypnotherapist.

2. The client must have the belief system that the change is possible.

Unlocking Past Blockages and Forgiveness

The person coming for hypnosis must absolutely be willing to accept the suggestions that he hypnotherapist gives him. This should not be difficult to accomplish since the hypnotherapist should be suggesting exactly what the client has asked him or her to suggest. However, many times there are past blockages, which must be unblocked or released before this acceptance can take place in the subconscious mind.

Blockages are usually created by hurt. We have all been hurt, emotionally and/or physically, by others many times during our lives. These hurts, whether they are real or perceived, are stored in our minds. They are memories connected to strong emotions, and they prevent us from moving on. Using hypnosis, we can go back to the original hurt and change our perception of it. Instead of seeing it as some awful truth, we can see it as a learning experience which helped us grow, but which no longer needs to effect us in the same way.

In cases where an individual has been physically and/or sexually abused, you may think it inappropriate to perceive it as a learning experience. We must, however, learn to change this perception and use it as a learning experience. In such cases, we generally must also give the victim back control.

When physical, sexual or even verbal abuse has occurred, the victim feels he or she had no control. These victims feel totally overpowered by the abuser. Using regression techniques, which we will discuss in greater detail later, we are able to return the victim to the various incidences, giving him power over the abuser. Once the victim reclaims control of the situation or incident, we are on the way to releasing the blockages.

A woman came to me a few years ago. She very much wanted to find a husband with whom she could spend the rest of her life. After many failed relationships, she was unable to make a commitment, even though she consciously wanted this more than anything else. During our discussion, I learned that her mother had died when she was about 8 years of age. Her father had beaten her before her mother's death, and afterwards, he began to abuse her sexually also.

Her father was now deceased, and consciously, she knew that he could never hurt her again. However, deep in her subconscious, the fears and emotions of that child still existed, and it was these fears and emotions that were stopping her from moving on with her life.

During the hypnosis session, I had her confront her father and tell him how much he had hurt her and how the scars were not only physical. There were deep emotional scars as well. I then offered her the opportunity to take control. I regressed her to just prior to the abuses, with her knowing what was about to happen, and I told her she now had the upper hand, and could stop him and punish him in any fashion she wanted. She chose to bring the police into the scene and have them arrest her father. After they took him away, she had him committed to a mental institution and had the key thrown away.

By imagining the above, the child in her had taken control and understood that she could not be hurt by her father again. I had her again talk to her father and forgive him for what he had done. With the understanding that she could now let go of all of those fears she had held on to for so long, she was able to forgive him. She was able to clear the past blockages that had up to that moment kept her from living her life to the fullest.

About a year later, she called me to tell me that she had met a wonderful man and was getting married. She had taken

21

control of her life and succeeded in getting what she really wanted.

Forgiveness

The most important step in releasing past blockages is forgiveness. If we cannot forgive, we cannot get on with our lives.

What is forgiveness? The word alone means, to absolve, or pardon. However, this absolution does not mean that we have to become friends with the one we are forgiving. It does not mean that they will not have to deal with the consequences of their actions. The reason forgiveness is necessary is so you can let go of the anger, the hatred, and all of the negative emotions that prohibit you from getting on with your life. Until you forgive, the person who hurt you (in whatever way) continues to live in your memory and emotions, and rent free at that, fostering negativity. What I am saying is, in order to move forward in your life, you must be filled with positives. You must work at using only positive words and having positive thoughts. Any negativity at all, in any area of your life, only sets up another hurdle in your path. Therefore, you must let go. You must forgive and let go. This also includes forgiving someone who is already dead. That memory is still causing problems and it also must be released.

One of my friends had a quote taped to the front of the

refrigerator as a reminder. It said "That which I focus on, I strengthen." As I pondered it, I realized how powerful a statement it really is. If you continually focus on the bad or negative side of someone or something, it will be the only part that you will be able to "see." However, if you focus on a positive about that person or thing, no matter how small that positive thing may be, it will immediately supersede all of the negatives. This is why forgiveness is necessary. With forgiveness you are allowing the negative to fade away in order that you can focus on the positive things in your life.

I know that it can be difficult to forgive, and I have had many clients tell me they have been hurt by someone so badly or that such an horrendous crime was committed, that they cannot forgive. I even had an elderly Jewish man ask me "Does this mean that I have to forgive Hitler?" My response was, "Absolutely! You don't have to forget him, because you never want such a thing to happen again. But you must forgive, because you must get on with your life."

I also explain to my clients that, if they have difficulty forgiving, they should "pretend" they forgive. I talked about the subconscious and pretending earlier. Pretending forgiveness is an example of how by pretending something, and by continuing to pretend, it will become reality.

Belief Systems

In order for permanent change to take place, you must believe that the change you desire is possible. A wonderful healer I met told me, "Believe-receive; doubt-do without." A simple, but extremely powerful statement. If you do not believe something is possible, it's not! It's as simple as that. On the other hand, if you believe something is possible, you can make it happen!

It is possible to effect change through hypnosis for someone who does not have the belief system that it will happen, but the results will be on shaky ground, and generally will not last. It would be like putting a Band-Aid on a deep cut that really needs stitches. In a few cases it may heal, but in most cases the cut will not close properly and will require further attention.

A dramatic case which really exemplifies how a belief system can make dramatic change, is that of a young boy I'll call Tommy. Tommy's mother called me as a last resort to help with her 12 year old son's temper. She explained that Tommy, at age 2, was diagnosed as having a degenerative optic nerve condition. As he got older his sight continued to worsen and he had been recently declared legally blind. He was a very sensitive child, and very proud. He refused to wear his glasses, which helped a little, and he would bump into people and things. Without his glasses he looked quite normal so when he bumped into someone, they would say something like, "Whattsa matter kid, you blind or something?" This would just aggravate Tommy's temper and he generally would lash out with his fists. He was sullen; he fought with his brother and even set a fire in his brother's room. His mother was at her wit's end.

I explained that hypnosis was indeed a good therapy for dealing with temper problems and arranged to meet with Tommy. On our first visit, as soon as Tommy's mom left the room (I insist on seeing the client without the parent, spouse or even close friend, in the room in, order to allow the client to express himself more freely and without feeling any inhibitions) Tommy said, "I know why I'm here, but, I know I am going to see again. Can you help me?" Although I was taken by surprise, I decided to pursue Tommy's question, since he had said it with such determination, and asked him how he knew he was going to see. He replied "I can see myself as being 16, and driving a car. I just know I'll be able to see again. Please, can you help me." I was confronted with a wonderfully positive belief system, so I told Tommy that I would see what we could do together once the hypnosis session began.

It turned out that Tommy was an excellent subject for hypnosis. He was able to let go, and very quickly and easily went into a very nicely relaxed state. We began our work. Since Tommy's mom had told me that he was diagnosed with his condition at age 2, I had a starting point and decided to regress Tommy to age 2 to see what had happened. It turned out that, from his crib, Tommy had seen his mother physically abused and raped. This was such a devastating scene for him that his subconscious mind closed down. If this is what he had to look at, he did not want to see!

We worked through the episode while he was in hypnosis. After the session, he opened his eyes and a remarkable improvement had taken place. When his mother came in, he looked at her and said "Mom, you have such pretty blue eyes!" His mother cried. Over the next few weeks, Tommy's vision continued to improve. His doctors were amazed. Tommy now has 20/20 vision with glasses.

This is a excellent example of how strong a belief system can be. If it weren't for Tommy's strong *belief* that he would see again, the above could not have happened.

To make this concept even more simple and understandable, consider times in your life when you felt you had a "cold coming on." The timing was terrible and you said to yourself, "I can't have a cold now, I don't have time for it." What happened? The cold never materialized. You *believed* that you would not get it and you didn't.

You are also dealing with that 10 year old subconscious mind that accepts everything as truth. It is the same emotional mind that reacts when you say to yourself every

Fall that "I get two colds every season." This belief sets up your subconscious mind to look for those two colds, and inevitably you get them.

Our belief systems are extremely powerful. To make incredible changes in our lives, all we must do is tap into a belief system and we've got it made.

CHAPTER 4 - STRESS & HEALTH

Most of us are aware of the connection between our mind and our bodies. Evidenced by the examples of belief in whether or not we will come down with a cold, or opening ourselves up for so many colds a season, this connection is mighty powerful.

As we juggle the demands of society today, we actually dream of eliminating stress from our lives. Elimination of stress is not the answer, but rather we should think in terms of harnessing its energies to our advantage. We must learn to control and reduce the amount of stress in our lives, as well as understand the role it plays in driving our thoughts and actions. We could not survive without stress; it is only when it is excessive and prolonged that it is harmful.

We are all familiar with the "fight or flight" syndrome of stress. However, when was the last time any of us has had to face the dangers of the hunt for our survival. Instead, we are overwhelmed by our work and responsibilities, and frustrated by the lack of time to get things done. In today's world the meaning of stress can be reduced to two words: Something unfinished. This could mean a decision that must be made, a letter that still must be written, a chore that must be done, an unresolved issue in a personal relationship, or even a phone call that must be returned. All of these represent something unfinished.

What then happens with the original feelings of fight or flight? Instead of our adrenaline rushing, forcing us to meet the enemy head on or run, we find ourselves pacing the floor, developing ulcers and/or headaches, or even muscle aches and pains. What happens when we are in a mentally stressful situation, and it continues for any length of time? Research has shown that when we are exposed to a stressful situation, it has profound effects on the body: Our breathing becomes shallow; our heart rate accelerates; our blood flow slows down; our muscles tense; our metabolism becomes rapid and erratic; and our hormones become imbalanced. Our body begins to break down at its weakest point. It is stress that is the underlying cause of most of our illnesses, the cause of our "dis-ease." Even illnesses we feel are caused by outside forces, such as viruses and other germs, are really given the go ahead to invade our bodies only when stress has taken a toll on our immune system and we can't fight them off.

By controlling our stress, we are truly taking charge of both our mental and physical health. We can actually ward off all sorts of ailments and illnesses. But, how can we control our stress?

Hypnosis is an easy and effective way to take hold of stress and release it before it can cause physical problems. By learning to relax and let go of the tension and fears caused by the stressful situation, we can actually become healthier and make our immune systems strong.

We know that hypnosis is a state of focused attention. Many of us focus on what is stressful in our lives, and become caught in the vicious cycle of continually reinforcing our disease. Yet, if we focus on something else, something soothing, we can relax our bodies and minds to create the feelings of happiness, balance and well-being that we so fervently desire.

But how do we attain the ideal of a totally relaxed, stress-free state? Using the techniques of self-hypnosis we focus on something that is totally non-threatening and totally neutral. This could be a favorite number or color. This change of focus allows us to push aside our negative preoccupations and fill our mind with feelings of peace and relaxation, leaving us balanced, centered, refreshed and revitalized -- ready to meet those unfinished tasks and unmade decisions head-on.

I always include programming for stress reduction with each and every session that I do. My preference is to use a favorite number, since a number never hurt anyone and is totally non-threatening. Using this favorite number as a trigger and a focus point, it provides the change in perception needed to bring the body and mind back into balance. With this returned balance, the physical responses follow: Breathing slows down; heart rate returns to normal; circulation increases; muscles relax; and the metabolism and hormones regain their equilibrium.

In the appendix I have included a script for stress reduction using a favorite number. Use it on yourself and experience how such a simple technique can keep you free of "dis-ease."

CHAPTER 5 - RELATIONSHIPS

It was a cold night in February. I was invited to a one man show at the Village Gate. Upon arrival, I learned the invitation was actually a sales ploy to get an audience -- all you had to do was pay the tax and buy two drinks.

Two tables away from me sat Cynthia and a friend. I overheard Cynthia talking about a pain in her shoulder, and as I walked by, I offered to help. I told her I was a hypnotist and could show her how to allow the pain to go away. I did a quick induction, made a suggestion and her pain disappeared. We exchanged business cards and I accepted her offer of a trade - hypnosis for a massage.

I had wonderful massage on the following Tuesday, and we made an appointment for a hypnotherapy session with her a week later. I asked her what she wanted, and she replied: "I'm forty years old. I've never been married, and now I want to be. I want a man for me -- the relationship that I have always known I would one day have." Her belief system was in place. This was going to be great!

At that session I did hypnosis with Cynthia to find that perfect relationship -- the man she was looking for to be her husband -- because that's exactly what she wanted.

That very evening just happened to be the first night of Passover and she was invited to a traditional Seder dinner with relatives and friends. At that dinner, Cynthia met Harry, a friend of a cousin. They hit it off, started dating and were married within three months.

WHY? HOW was this woman, after an excess of 20 years of trying to find this kind of happiness, now able to find the right person in just a matter of hours? How did the hypnosis allow the situation to take place?

After years of trying to make this happen, why did it happen now? Because she stopped trying and just went out there and did it! The hypnotherapy session, which took 2½ hours went like this:

Because Cynthia felt comfortable with me, having met with me on two prior occasions, I already had the rapport necessary to get her into a very relaxed state quite effortlessly. After another 15 minutes of relaxation, which was necessary for the reinforcement tape I was making for her, I proceeded to do regression back to her childhood. By using the memory, as well as having her focus on feelings in the body, I brought her back to 7 years of age on a day that she did not feel that wonderful. It was a day her father and mother had just had an argument. Apparently it was nothing dramatic, just a little tiff which happened infrequently, as her parents enjoyed a relatively good marriage. Bringing her back to that scene just minutes after the argument, Cynthia was helping her mother with the dishes. Her mother, in a jokingly way, said to Cynthia

33

"Don't ever fall in love with a man. They're just not worth it and just cause you pain and unhappiness." The emotional mind (subconscious) had no way to distinguish this statement any other way than as a true statement. In other words, what went into the little girls memory bank that day was, "If I ever fall in love with man, all I will get in return is pain and unhappiness." NOT wanting that pain and unhappiness, she was programmed from that moment on never to fall in love.

People do things for two reasons: 1) to avoid pain and 2) to gain pleasure. By planting in the subconscious not to fall in love, it was simply perceived, by that 7 year old girl, that she has now avoided pain and this allowed her to feel good. The mother put that myth there and it is the mother that can also take it away. Working with that childlike mind, I went on to tell her that what her mother did was perhaps a necessary venting for her mother at that time and she just happened to be there, open and vulnerable. It was a "learning experience" and a valuable lesson at that time. I suggested she was glad for experience, but now it's no longer necessary to hold on to it.

I then had her go through a forgiveness process. By forgiving her mother and father and anyone else who ever hurt that child or childlike emotions of the adult, real or perceived. I had her forgive them one at a time, and then had her forgive her inner child for all of the guilt she put herself through in past years. After all, all of those relationships she may have had up until this moment may have caused guilt because she could not "fall in love." She had to forgive all. All of the energy in the body had to flow evenly and positively.

Now we were ready to do the programming. With all the negativity removed, I first filled her with self-confidence (no matter what a person comes to the hypnotist for, what they really want is self-confidence), motivation, joy and happiness. Then, I had her pretend she was actually in this wonderful relationship. This was done through feelings and emotions, not by seeing a particular person. It is the conscious mind that discriminates by looks, by profession, etc. The subconscious mind reacts to the emotions and feelings of the relationship.

Since the subconscious mind doesn't know the difference between reality and fantasy, we allowed her to believe that she was already involved in the relationship that she really wanted. I then asked her how she felt in this relationship. She replied: "Excited, comfortable, secure, playful, loving, and tingling in upper part of my legs." Then I turned on the machine and recorded those same words into her reinforcement tape. I explained to her conscious mind that, unless she gets those feelings, she will just keep moving on. When she meets the right person, she will get those feelings first.

I then did more positive programing stressing that she

deserves love, deserves happiness, deserves to be married, etc. The key word is "deserves."

As stated, Cynthia found the love of her life that very night. After two weeks, she realized it was real and called the dating service she had registered with and asked to be removed from the list. She had found the love she was looking for. When she explained that she had been programmed by a hypnotherapist, they called me to get more information.

I made an appointment to see dating service people a week later and hypnotized one of their employees, a woman named Susan. After having been divorced for more than 10 years she found a great relationship two days later. More noticeable to her was the way she interacted with men. She enrolled in my hypnotherapy certification course and began doing this type of programming in conjunction with her work. This, in turn, led to speaking engagements for me, and the secret was out.

Sally Jessy Raphael featured me on her show, which produced over 900 phone calls to my office, and brought me clients from all over the world. I became consistently busy with clients who believed that they could now find their perfect mate. Amazingly, most of the sessions were working and the results were nothing less than astounding. One client met her future husband five minutes after leaving the session when she went to get a cab. Another client who came in from Wisconsin, met her true love in the elevator of my office building. The gentleman happened to be from Chicago and after a month of dating they became engaged.

Why does this programming work? Getting into bad relationships or no relationships at all is caused by our past programming (as illustrated above with Mom telling Cynthia "Don't fall in love, men are not worth it!"). Whether it's been programming to avoid the relationship, or programming that we are not worthy, it has created blockages that prevent finding and attracting that perfect person we so desire to have in our lives. They are prevented by fear. Whether it's fear of success or fear of failure in the relationship, it is induced fear. Once we understand at the subconscious level that we are deserving of, and that it is okay to be successful in a relationship, amazing transformations can take place.

Another blockage created by our conscious mind, is the one which discriminates against looks, employment, education, etc. This conscious discrimination obscures the emotions that we are seeking in a true relationship. Again, the subconscious mind must be accessed and programmed to understand that how another person makes us feel is the true key, not the superficial requirements of the critical conscious mind.

Remember, we act to avoid pain or to gain pleasure. In seeking a relationship we must focus more on the pleasurable, i.e. the "feelings" that a true and loving relationship will bring, rather that the fear of a bad relationship. Back to the note on the refrigerator, "That which I focus on I strengthen." Focus on the deserving part that is ready for that wonderful relationship and be ready to receive.

CHAPTER 6 - SUCCESS & SELF-CONFIDENCE

No matter what the primary, conscious reason for the client's visit to the hypnotherapist, success and self-confidence are the bottom line.

We all need that pat on the back once in a while. The pleasure gained from that pat surmounts the fears of failures. Through hypnosis self-confidence can be developed through the release and clearing of the blockages. It can then be heightened through imagining the feelings that success and self-confidence instill in us.

To illustrate how that pat on the back really can make a profound difference, consider the case of the little blind boy named Stevie Morris. In school, Stevie was very shy, rarely spoke, and was very insecure. He was in a standard grade school class where all his fellow classmates were sighted. He felt different, and lacked the confidence to make friends. One day a mouse was loose in the classroom, and it was causing general chaos. Although everyone was doing their best to catch the mouse, they were having little success since the mouse could easily hide. The teacher asked Stevie for his help. Stevie could not understand why the teacher was asking him, a blind boy who could not even see the mouse, for help. The teacher explained: "Stevie, because you are unable to see, you have learned to hear much better than the rest of us. I'll bet you are able to hear the mouse moving around. Will you please listen hard and tell us where the mouse is so that we can catch it?" Stevie listened, and located the mouse, which was quickly caught and put out of the classroom. He was the hero of the day! This incident changed Stevie's life. He learned that he had special talents, which others could admire. His school work improved, and he began to make friends. He became more confident each day. That same little Stevie Morris grew up to become a top musician, performer and songwriter, calling himself Stevie Wonder!

Once self-confidence is developed, success programming is the next step. At this point, I cannot stress enough how removing the blockages in our subconscious is key to making real change. A good example of this can be seen from the work I did with a student of mine, whose name is Gerard.

During my hypnotherapy training classes I, generally, use students as volunteers for demonstration sessions. Gerard volunteered on one such occasion, stating that he really wanted programming for success and self-confidence. He explained, in front of the entire class that, although he had a good job in the sales field and was making a respectable living, he was not able to break through his self-limiting barriers to become the super-salesman he felt he could be. We went to work.

As we began the interactive part of the session, I began to look for the blockages which might be keeping Gerard from the success he desired. While leading him through a confrontation with his mother, the major blockage was uncovered. Being a black man from South Carolina, Gerard's mother had always told him, "Son, you're a good boy and you're smart. You'll be good at whatever you do, but you'll never have what 'whitey' has." In this simple statement, she imposed her perceived limitations on her son. Although she felt that she was being realistic and truthful, as well as keeping her son from being hurt, she actually put a limit on his success.

As we continued the session, I had Gerard release this block and forgive his mother, and then we went on to the programming part of the session. I have kept in contact with Gerard, who succeeded in becoming top salesperson for his company. His confidence boosted, he actually went on to start his own company, which is off the ground and growing nicely. His blocks gone, Gerard continues to have increasing confidence in his abilities, and he has been able to accept the success he deserves.

We all have put limitations on ourselves, as Gerard did, and we must overcome them in order to achieve our own success. My original hypnosis instructor, Steven LaVelle, stressed that "You can never be more than your expectations." If you do not expect to be successful, you will not be successful. You have placed a limitation upon yourself. But, through hypnosis, you can actually go back and reprogram yourself to lift those limitations.

One way to experience reaching beyond your limitations is to do a "Fire Walk." After spending 3 hours with the group and then walking with bare feet over white-hot coals, without getting burned, is a true test of reaching beyond expectations and changing belief systems. If you can change the energy of your body so the heat of the burning coals does not harm you, you can pretty much conquer any obstacle standing in the way of your success.

Another important step towards success is the development of a "success consciousness." Too many of us find ourselves in a rut, in a job we do not particularly care for, and complain constantly about not having opportunities to move forward. We "if only" ourselves to death. "If only" I had worked harder; "If only" my boss understood how hard I work; "If only" I could get promoted; "If only" this, "If only" that. This consciousness is the consciousness of failure. We must change it to success consciousness.

An example of how perception changes attitude, is that of a waitress in a diner nearing the end of her shift. It's been a long day and she's tired. A whole bus load of people arrive. How she perceives this event will determine how she experiences it. If she looks at all of those passengers as ruining the possibility of her leaving on time and causing her to feel more tired than she already is, she will resent them. This in turn will cause her to emit negative energy, which in turn will create unhappy, negative customers. On the other hand, if she looks at this group coming in as an opportunity to help these passengers get the nourishment they need to continue on their journey, and the chance to make some more tips, she will give off positive energy, making her job easier, and making the entire situation happier and more pleasing for her customers.

Too many people act as if they are robots, not really caring about the job they are doing, or the other people they are working for or with. Success consciousness means doing your particular job with a positive attitude and to the best of your ability. By creating a flow of positive energy from yourself, by caring about what you are doing, you will create a success consciousness which can take you beyond those self-imposed limitations. Change your thoughts and your energy and your actions change along with them.

CHAPTER 7 - CHANGING THE CONSCIOUSNESS, CHANGING THE ENERGY

I've given you examples of "You get back what you put out." I've illustrated how focusing on the positive highlights the positive, and focusing on the negative highlights the negative. Now let's look at how positive and negative energy affect us.

We are all energy. Everything around us is energy. It is only the density of that energy that gives shape and form to the living and inanimate things around us. Without even thinking about it, we all recognize and react to the energy around us. Have you ever walked into a room where "the atmosphere is so thick you could cut it with a knife?." This certainly implies a less than friendly feeling. On the other hand, have you ever walked into a room and just felt good? It could have been the colors, the aromas, the sounds. You were responding to the energy.

Have you ever been in a room when you all of a sudden "felt" someone as staring at you. Then, you turned around and sure enough someone was. It was the energy of that person to which you were responding. It was the energy of his or her thoughts and being.

We also give off positive and negative energy, depending upon our thoughts and our feelings. What we must learn is how to change the energy we are giving off to the most positive and the most confident. This is what I do for my clients in each and every private hypnotherapy session. In order to successfully change themselves and their behavior, there must be a change in their energy.

We can effectively change both behavior and emotions to reflect the positive through hypnosis by accessing the subconscious mind where permanent behavioral change can be made. The energy is also effectively changed by doing this.

Many times you can determine someone's mood just by looking. Posture and facial expression are certain giveaways to how we feel, whether it is happy, sad, peaceful, angry, tired, energetic, etc. The energy of each of these is different and feels different both to the individual and to those around him.

An easy way to experience a change in energy is to simply shift your position. Try it. If you are sitting and reading this, just shift your position to straight back, shoulders back and feet flat on the floor. If you are lying down, shift to a more upright position, with neck and back straighter and shoulders back. Now notice how this change in position makes you feel. You have become more alert, more aware. You have created an energy change.

Next time you are feeling a bit low, or not very confident, try changing your posture or position. You'll find that this simple trick can make a huge difference on your outlook, and also on the way others look at you. You will feel better and more confident, and you will appear confident and in control. You will be sending off a new set of signals that those around you will respond to in a more positive way, all with a simple change of posture. Now, at the same time you shift position, allow your mind to focus on feeling terrific and feeling confident, and you'll really have something good going for you.

Remember, don't just read this and file it in the back of your mind. Practice it! Notice the difference in the way you respond to others and the way they respond to you! You'll be amazed!

The same concept holds true for letting go of our self-imposed limitations. If we are constantly telling ourselves the only way to get ahead is to work hard, we will find ourselves "working very hard." On the other hand, if we are always telling ourselves work is fun, and getting ahead is a matter of being focused and organized, we will find ourselves becoming more successful through this focus and organization, and getting ahead while having a lot of fun.

Because you get back what you put out there, let's continue to focus on what you are putting out, and then let's reframe it. To begin, it is necessary to make a list of your beliefs about success and prosperity and then to reframe it with a positive consciousness. For example, if you currently believe "It is difficult to make ends meet in this economy," your must reword or reframe your statement to "It's easy for me to make money in this economy." Or, if you think "It's difficult to make the right decisions to get ahead," you can change it to "I always make the right decisions." A simple statement on the job such as "I hate dealing with my supervisor on this matter," creates in itself the drudgery of the act. Next time you find yourself beginning to think "I hate" doing a particular task, immediately change it to "I love" and continue the sentence. You will find that just by saying the words -- even if you don't mean it -- makes the task or situation easier. And, the more you change this thought pattern, the more you change the energy of the task or situation, and the easier it becomes!

By making these lists, and by changing your words and your thought patterns, you will change your consciousness and change your energy. You will truly bring only the best to yourself. It is all there for you. In fact, when you begin doing this, it is not even necessary to believe what you are saying. The more you do it, the more believable it becomes, until the positives are firmly planted in your mind.

Remember, each time you find yourself entertaining a limiting thought immediately change the words in your mind to a wonderful and positive statement. Simply by changing the thought, the attitude and energy change along with it!

CHAPTER 8 - PRETEND, PRETEND, PRETEND

Let's get back to that 10-year-old, emotional, subconscious mind that we all have, and to how this subconscious does not understand the word pretend. I've explained that by changing our thoughts, we can change our energy, even without the belief system at first. This is called "pretending." Let's examine pretending some more.

As children, pretending was easy for us. Our imagination was wide open and our learning curve was steep. We loved to pretend we were grown up; to pretend we were cowboys and Indians; to pretend we were superheros. As we pretended and while we pretended, we became, even though just for a short while, who we were pretending to be. We actually took on another persona and in some cases even felt we were invincible. As we got older, our parents made us more and more aware of the difference between reality and fantasy. In many cases, as we got older, our pretending was actually discouraged by our parents. They actually put limits (again with the limits) on our fantasizing, telling us we had to accept reality. Our ability to pretend began to diminish until as adults, we probably stopped pretending altogether.

In reality, pretending is healthy and can extremely be beneficial to us. As I demonstrated in the earlier self-hypnosis exercise, by pretending to feel terrific, you may have actually begun to feel that way. When I talked about forgiveness, I explained that if you can't really forgive a person, pretend to forgive. That pretending to forgive, is actually a form of letting go, and can be beneficial, for the more we pretend to forgive, the easier it becomes, and eventually we really do learn to forgive.

These examples deal with changes in emotions or feelings, but let's look at how pretending can actually help us achieve success. Say there is something you really want to accomplish, but you have fears about it. For instance, pretend you are a computer salesman with an opportunity to make an important sales presentation to XYZ Company, a company on the verge of making a huge changeover in hardware and software. This sale could mean the commission of a lifetime. You are excited and begin planning the presentation. But as you do, fears and doubts begin to surface. You think: "Why should this company want to listen to me? They are probably checking out the biggest companies in the business, what makes me think that they'll want my products?"

The negativity has set in, and the hurdles and road blocks have been put in place. Now what happens? You must find away around all of the obstacles you have placed in your own way. You have made this a very difficult task.

Here's where a change in your perception of the entire situation can mean the difference between the road to success or the road to failure. It can be done through a simple process of thinking backwards. Instead of focusing on why XYZ Company <u>won't</u> buy from you, let's **pretend** that you've already made the sale. Wow! You've just made the sales coup of the century! You've made the deal of all deals and the commission of all commissions. You are on cloud nine, walking on air! You're the hit of your company and every other sales person's idol. **Imagine it! Feel it! Sense it all over!** Describe to yourself exactly what your emotions are, how you feel physically, how you see this successful you in the mirror!

Now that you know you've done it, you've made the sale, let's look back and see how you did it. This is where the thinking backwards comes in. This is a total change in your perception of the situation. Instead of seeing all of the obstacles in your way, you can "look back" at the process of the sale. You can see and know how you made that perfect presentation, with such self-confidence, and knowledge about your product. Instead of focusing on the negatives, you can go with all of the positives that moved your presentation forward and helped you make the sale.

With this confidence and this knowledge, due to pretending, you have changed your energy. You now know that you will be successful, and your confidence and ability will show in that important presentation, allowing you to do the very best possible job you can do.

By pretending and thinking backwards we can actually

overcome many of the negatives that previously stopped us from moving forward in most any situation. Allow yourself to pretend you've accomplished a specific goal or task. Allow yourself to experience that win. Allow yourself to experience it with all of your senses. When you can pretend and experience the success, you can really do it!

CHAPTER 9 - TRYING IS LYING

I would like to see the word "try" removed from the English language. What does it mean to "try." If you "try," does that mean you succeed? Absolutely not. In fact, the word trying implies not completing the task. "I tried," generally brings along with it the words, "but I failed."

If you invite someone to a party, and that person says "I'll try to make it," I'd bet money that person didn't show. Let's not "try." Let's (as Nike so aptly puts it) just do it! Let's just eliminate that word "try."

The sister word of "try" is "hope." It may seem appropriate to say "There's always hope," to someone in a grave situation or with a serious illness, but think about when you use it. You use this when there really is no hope. If you say, "I hope" something will happen, you are saying that you have nothing to do with the outcome. Isn't it better to think "I'm going to do my best to make it happen!" Now you are applying positive action and positive energy.

Next time you are tempted to use the word "try," change it to "I'll do my best." Next time you want to use the word hope, change it to "I'm certain." You have changed your position from negative to positive with this simple rewording. You have also put yourself in charge and have changed the energy around you. You have used a simple phrase to move from failure to success.

Remember the popular children's story of "The Little Engine that Could." What a success image for children. "I think I can; I think I can; I <u>know</u> I can." If we, as adults, focused on those simple worlds "I think I can," or "I know I can," rather than "I'll try," imagine how much more successful we would be. This is really self-hypnosis. Our attention is focused, and the emotions of the "I can" allow us to access our subconscious mind where we can impact positive behavioral change.

What we all must do is become more childlike, keep things simple, focus on the positive, and we're there! We can do it!

CHAPTER 10 - FEARS AND PHOBIAS

Hypnotherapy and self-hypnosis are also effective ways to deal with fears and phobias. One of the interesting things I've noticed in my hypnotherapy practice is that people's fears are usually, although not always, based upon something experienced by someone other than themselves.

For example, many people afraid of dogs, were taught this fear by a parent or sibling, or a respected adult who told them a story of how a dog had hurt them. This in turn reached their emotions and they became afraid without ever really experiencing the feared incident.

I once heard a story which is a good example of fearing something imagined but not experienced: During World War II, two Americans were captured. The enemy slit the wrists of one man, and the other was forced to watch the slow death, and then it would be his turn. What happened was, the prisoner watching actually died first. He had not experienced anything himself, but was instead shown what he imagined *might* happen to him. He died from his imagined fear alone.

The difference between a fear and a phobia is that a fear is rational, while a phobia is irrational. The fear of lion or tiger is rational, while fear of a house kitten is irrational. It is also possible for a real fear to become an irrational phobia. I had a client who happened to be a bit on the obsessive side about cleanliness. However, because of a series of experiences, she actually became phobic about dirt to the point that she was so afraid of the "dirt" that she would not allow another person to touch her. When she came to my office, she would not put her coat down or even give it to anyone for fear that it might drop on the floor, and then she would not be able to wear it. Her fear of "dirt" was not allowing her to live any kind of life. She had no friends, because no one could touch her. She isolated herself in order not to come in contact with dirt, and no one could come to her home because they might bring in dirt. If something spilled on the floor, she could barely wipe it up for fear of getting more dirt on herself. Through hypnosis we got to the cause of her problem.

This client was physically abused by her ex-husband every day of her 3-year marriage. However, as we proceeded through this problem, it was apparent that whatever was the cause, came before her marriage. It was finally revealed that when she arrived in the United States from Puerto Rico at the age of 19, her uncle, whom she respected and was somewhat dependent on, told her she was possessed by spirits. He further convinced her that the only way to get rid of these spirits would be to have oral sex with him. Being naive, alone and afraid, she submitted to her uncle. However, once she realized that she had been duped by him, she told him over and over and he was "lower than dirt." The emotions of the abuse, connected with the word dirt, changed her somewhat overly zealous cleanliness into a true phobia. Once she was able to establish the reason for her abnormal fear in her 10 year old emotional mind, she was able to return to a more normal life. In fact, when she left the session, she hugged me and several of my students. This is something she could not have done 2 hours before.

Another client came to me because she failed her driving test five times. She could pass the written test with ease, but each time she would get behind the wheel for the actual driving part, she would become so fearful, she would actually experience a panic attack and fail. During the hypnosis session, she told me about her family, and about her grandfather. The day that her grandfather got his driver's license, he hit a young boy with the car and killed him. This story had made such an impact on her that she was unable to relax behind the wheel of the car long enough to pass a driving test. Using hypnotherapy and reprogramming, she was able to pass her driving test that week.

Many people are "afraid" to speak to a group of people. In fact, a group of college students was polled. The results of the poll showed that more students were afraid of public speaking that they were of death. Imagine, according to this, these student would actually prefer death over speaking in public. This fear does not seem realistic.

What we must understand is that fear is a feeling. It is not an action. As noted earlier, in most cases, it is not even based on anything we have actually experienced. It is a feeling connected to an emotion. It is the focus on that feeling and emotion that causes the problems. To correct it or get rid of the fear, we must change the focus, which in turn changes the feeling and the emotions. We can then confront the feared person, place or thing with that changed focus, and what we get is a totally different reaction.

Let's go back to that person who is afraid of dogs. I can hypnotize that person and have them confront the fear. However, while in hypnosis, and while imagining confronting this feared dog, I have the person look at the dog and see it change into a cute, little cartoon puppy. I ask the person if he is now afraid of this cartoon puppy. If he responds no, it is not threatening at all, I can now work with the person on overcoming the fear of dogs. Each time he imagines being confronted by a dog, he watches it as it turns into a harmless cartoon, and each confrontation becomes easier and easier, until the fear subsides because dogs are no longer threatening to him.

We can also work through fears with self-hypnosis by pretending, of course. This is especially helpful in dealing with a fear such as fear of public speaking. One easy way is to use the process of thinking backwards. Imagine yourself as having made the speech or presentation, and imagine how delighted the audience is. Allowing this picture of a successful presentation to go around and around in your mind, using self-hypnosis, can build confidence.

Then when the moment comes to stand up for the speech or presentation, you can change your focus to that neutral, unthreatening favorite number or color that you use to reduce stress. This change of focus, eliminates the physical symptoms of stress, so that we can now go on with the show (so to speak) in a cool, calm and collected manner, using positive energy. Fear is thus eliminated.

We can all relate to the bully we knew in school. The fear of the bully was generally based upon his actions with perhaps one or two children. He then took advantage of his reputation, usually through attitude alone, until most all of the children feared him. However, all it took was for one determined person to stand up to the bully, and show that the reputation was really based on a very weak foundation. Once confronted, the feared object is reduced to reality, not emotion.

Once we face the fear, determine its true cause, and change the emotion associated with it, we've won the battle!

CHAPTER 11 - YOUR INNER CHILD

I have stressed the fact that it is the 10-year-old emotional, subconscious mind we must access in order to make behavioral change. I have also stressed that forgiveness is the key to letting go of past blockages. Now let's look at the need to connect with that 10-year-old child and apply forgiveness to that child.

I believe inner child work is necessary in every case, in every session. No matter what the blockage or hurt, or the age when it happend, there is always guilt. Everyone who has ever come to me for a session, no matter what the situation, has always expressed some guilt for either having done something wrong or not having done something right. This has even held true in the cases of random attack or rape. There is always a sense of guilt.

In order to release the blockage and let go of it, that inner child must understand that whatever the situation, it was a learning experience for which there should be no guilt. Therefore forgiveness of the child is necessary. To do this, I have my clients imagine that child within them. I have them take that child in their arms and hold it. They forgive the child for anything the child may or may not have done and they talk to that child telling the child how much he or she is loved and protected. It is through this act of actual self-forgiveness that real healing begins. This simple act makes a huge difference in the mental and emotional healing of the client. After all, if we cannot love and respect ourselves, starting with the child within us, how can we possibly love and respect others.

Our inner child holds the key to our peace of mind, our self-respect, our self-esteem and our confidence. By building up that inner child, by learning love and respect for ourselves, and by changing our consciousness about ourselves, we are then able to make the most incredible changes in our lives.

I've included a wonderful inner-child script in the appendix which you can record for yourself. Do it! It's a wonderful experience.

CHAPTER 12 - FIND THE CAUSE

In all of the situations I have given as examples up to this point, permanent change became possible only when the underlying cause of the problem was isolated and dealt with on the subconscious level. From unlocking blockages, which referred to the "cause" of the hurts we all have experienced, to confronting the bully in school, change came only when we confronted the hurt, the issue or the emotion, and really examined it for what it was.

Here's where the hypnotherapist differs from the general hypnotist. Most hypnotists will talk with the client, determine what change the client wishes to make and then give a direct suggestion for that change to be made. If the client wishes to lose weight, the hypnotist will make specific suggestions about feeling satisfied by eating smaller amounts of food, and making healthier choices, etc. If the client wants to stop biting nails, the suggestion will be made that the desire to bite the nails has disappeared, and so on. Since each and every one of us accepts suggestion differently, depending on our state of mind and our beliefs, the suggestion given may last an hour, a day, a week, a month, a year, or a lifetime. We can never be certain. In most of these instances of simple direct suggestion, the hypnotist has merely put a band aid on the problem. This band aid is put on without cleaning and disinfecting the wound. It is possible that, if the wound was a minor one, the Band-Aid will take care of the situation. In most cases, however, since the infection was not treated, the wound continues to fester and your are right back where you started.

To heal the wound, it must be treated and cleansed before putting on the Band-Aid. This is what the hypnotherapist does. He finds the cause of the wound or problem, confronts it and changes perception of it (cleansing), and then fills the wound by putting in new positive and healing energy (treatment).

To illustrate, I had a client who had been on every diet every out there, but was unable to let go of unwanted weight. She would eat without knowing what she was tasting, or even what she was eating in many cases. During her hypnotherapy session with me, I asked her to go back to the first time she experienced eating like this. She began to talk about her parents, and how they always were fighting at the dinner table. She would not say a word, but would just continue putting food into her mouth until the argument was over, or she was excused. Her eating behavior was a direct reaction to the unpleasant quarreling and it became a habit. It kept her mouth full and busy so that she did not have to respond to a difficult, unpleasant situation. Once she allowed herself to understand her behavior and its cause, she was able to stop the behavior and let go of the weight.

There are several ways to get to the cause of a behavioral or emotional problem. One way is through hypnotic regression, as in the above example. Another way is to focus on a bodily feeling, which can take the mind and the emotions directly to a particular situation. Sometimes we even find that sounds and smells will trigger specific reactions, based on something that happened in conjunction with that particular sound or smell. Through hypnosis, we then reframe the situation so that the ten year old emotional, subconscious mind can understand the reactions to those triggers are no longer necessary.

Finding the cause of an emotional or behavioral problem is as important as finding the cause of a mechanical problem. For instance, if the air in your car tires keeps escaping, you can do two things. You can either keep putting more and more air in, or you can find the cause, or hole in the tire and repair it. By putting in more air all the time, you are merely treating a symptom which will keep reappearing. By finding the hole, you are going to the cause and mending it so the problem ceases.

Finding the cause of the mental, emotional or behavioral problem, allows mending to take place so that the symptoms cease to exist. Permanent change is then made.

CHAPTER 13 - WEIGHT LOSS WITH HYPNOSIS

Weight loss is one area where hypnosis is extremely effective. We all know that diets don't work. What really works is behavior modification, and hypnosis is a key to modifying behavior effortlessly.

One of the reasons diets don't work is that the 10-year-old subconscious mind does not understand "cutting down." That 10-year-old child, only understands deprivation, and cutting down means deprivation. A 10-year-old does not want to be deprived.

Another phenomenum happens when we tell someone we "lost 10 pounds." The subconscious mind picks up this message and says, "She lost 10 pounds? I'd better go out and find them! I'd better add a few more just in case she loses them again!"

When we think in terms of becoming fit and trim, we should think in terms of "letting go" of unwanted or unnecessary weight. "Letting go" sends a positive signal to the subconscious. There is no need to go out and replace something that was "lost."

Once we find the cause and clear the blockages we can begin the positive work of "letting go." One particular client, whose name is Vickie, has had incredible success using hypnosis to let go of 80 unwanted and unnecessary pounds. Vickie, once very trim and fit, began to experience back trouble, eventually undergoing 3 different back surgeries to correct disk problems. She was bedridden, with nothing to do but eat and watch television. Her husband would leave for work each day, putting all sorts of food and snacks by her bedside, along with the television remote control. Her life became eating and watching television. Instead of getting better, she gained weight, her muscle tone deteriorated and walking became more and more painful. The doctors predicted that eventually she would be confined to a wheel chair, never to walk again. They offered her no hope.

Vickie lives outside of Charlotte, NC, and it was the experiences surrounding Hurricane Hugo that changed her life and led her to hypnotherapy. The effects of Hugo were devastating for her. She was alone at home during the storm, and a tree came right into her house. After the event, she was a physical and mental wreck. She was still an invalid. She was afraid to be home alone. She was afraid of storms. She was so nervous she didn't know what to do. Then someone from her church gave her a relaxation tape. She responded so well to the tape and felt so much better that she decided to look into hypnosis as a means to help physically and mentally. She heard about the seminar that I was conducting in North Carolina and made arrangements to attend with a friend. That weekend truly changed her life.

I hypnotized her during the workshop, and we learned the cause of her problems was that she never felt accepted by her parents. It was only a short time before this session that she learned the father she always knew was not her biological father. At least now she understood why she always had those feelings. She was able to release the negative feelings and to forgive. Within 9 months time she had let go of 80 pounds. She went from a size 22 to a size 10. Her back was better, she was exercising regularly by walking and doing water aerobics, and she felt better than she'd felt since she was a teenager. She began to enjoy her young grandson, and was ecstatic about living a normal life once again.

Vickie was so impressed with her own response, she decided that she wanted to help others make similar changes. She is her own walking commercial, and has opened her own successful hypnosis center outside of Charlotte.

I've heard Oprah Winfrey talking to her viewers on television and to readers of her books on how holding on to anger and resentment were the main cause of her holding on to excess weight. She has told her audiences that once she realized that all the while she was spending her time and energy being angry at others, they were going on with their lives totally unaffected by her anger and resentment, she finally let it go. That mental and emotional release also released all those pounds.

In my practice I have noticed that, generally, when a woman is extremely obese and over a period of many years has not been able to make any headway whatsoever in letting go of those excess pounds through diet and hypnosis done by direct suggestion only, I find a situation where physical or sexual abuse has occurred. The excess pounds were put there to form a protective shield. The subconscious feels that, if I am overweight, I will not be attractive and therefore I will not be a target for sexual activity. It is only when that woman deals with the abuse and the abuser, by finding the cause, taking control and then forgiving, that the weight finally begins to come off and real change is made. Therefore, if you are very obese, and are seeking a hypnotherapist to help you in this area, please make certain you find one who has the proper training and credentials to help you find the real cause and then assist you to work through it and release it. Remember, we need to heal the wound, not just put a Band-Aid over it. Once you can let go of the cause, you can win your battle with the bulge!

CHAPTER 14 - PAST LIFE! IS IT REAL?

Much has been written in recent years on past life therapy. We could argue until we are blue in the face, and still no one will ever prove whether there is or there is not past life experience. In hypnotherapy the proof of the existence is not necessary, because it's the belief system that counts, and past life therapy works!

It is a therapy, and it is used to find "the cause" of a physical, mental or emotional problem which elicits an unwanted behavior. I have two particular cases which are excellent examples of how the key to changing a behavior was found in a past life.

A woman came to me because it seemed like every time her husband, who was a chiropractor, had to go out of town on business, her back went out. She couldn't explain it. It just happened. There appeared to be no reason for this to happen, it just did. In the hypnotherapy session, there appeared to be no physical "cause" for this to happen. The problem began after her marriage, and there was no incident that she could remember which could be a trigger for this problem. Since she had already indicated during our preliminary discussion that she believed in past life, I decided to explore this avenue.

What came up, during the past life session, was a lifetime when she was a Native American woman and her current husband was also her husband in that life. It seems that she and her husband were very much in love and very spiritually connected; they were what we refer to now as "twin flames." One day, her husband went off to hunt, leaving her behind in the village. While he was gone, the village was attacked and the inhabitants were massacred. She took a spear in the back and was dying when her husband returned, unaware, to the village. He found her, and held her in his arms as she died. She described feeling terrible guilt and hurt because she was leaving him behind. She wanted to cling to him and never leave him.

Now that she understood why her back would go out when her husband would go away on business, it never happened again. There is no longer a need to repeat the pain in this lifetime.

Another woman came to me complaining of severe asthma. She had stopped smoking several months before, but her breathing problem had deteriorated to the point that she could last 2 hours without her inhaler. During the hypnosis session I regressed her, but she could not find a time in this lifetime when she did not have the problem. As in the last example, I had already determined that she had a belief in past life. I had her focus on her chest, the feelings and emotions going on there and she immediately went to a past life, to the first asthma attack she had ever had. She was a 22 year old woman with two children. Her husband loved her, but could not tolerate the children. He would become extremely agitated by them, causing him to scream and yell. This upset her terribly to the point that she could not breathe. This breathing difficulty developed into the asthma, which would change his focus from the children to take care of her.

Now that she knew how the problem began, she could go about changing the perception of it. It was no longer needed in this lifetime and she allowed it to disappear. She has not had an asthma attack since this session.

As mentioned, both of these women had indicated a belief in past life prior to being hypnotized. I simply used their own belief systems to assist them in finding a reason or cause for their problem, and in finding a way to relieve it. I am not suggesting this will work for everyone, but it will work for those who believe.

Another dramatic example of how dealing with a past life problem helped in this life, is that of a young 16 year old South African girl who attended one of my seminars. She was a very unhappy young woman, but seemed very interested in hypnosis and was doing well in the workshop. As I read the cards I have the workshop attendees complete, listing the behaviors they would like to change, I came upon her's saying she wanted to get rid of her desire to commit suicide. When her parents arrived to take her home that evening, I asked to speak with them. They expressed deep concern about her, and indicated that she was constantly depressed and had even stopped going to school. Because she seemed to respond to me and hypnosis, they agreed to bring her for a session.

The next day her mother brought her to see me. She spoke about her inability to communicate with her parents and began telling me how often her father hit her. She then said "Don't think he abuses me. He doesn't. I hit him first all the time and continue hitting him until he finally hits back." When I questioned her why she would hit her father, she didn't know. She would just lose control when with him and would lash out at him with her fists.

She turned out to be a wonderful hypnosis subject. While focusing on the emotions she felt around her father, she immediately went back into a past life in Nazi Germany. The story that unfolded cast her as a bar girl and her father, from this life, was a Nazi soldier. She was raped and violated, and spoke about having her eyes torn out. However, just before her eyes were torn out, she realized that it was her father, as the Nazi soldier, who did this to her.

We went through the process of understanding that her anger towards him was no longer necessary in this life. We went through the healing process, and she was able to forgive him for what he had done to her. She left the session a changed person.

71

When I returned to South Africa 6 months later, I didn't recognize her when she appeared at one of my seminars. She was absolutely beautiful. She had gone back to school, made new friends and had even begun modeling. She was smiling and happy. Her parents were thrilled. Family life was wonderful because she was getting along with her father. She was an entirely different person.

If you believe you have had a past life, or perhaps are just curious about the possibility, I have included a past life script in the appendix which you can read and record and play back to take a gentle journey to a past life. Don't knock it until you've tried it!

CHAPTER 15 - HYPNOSIS AND HEALING

"When you can't remember why you're hurt, that's when you're healed. When you have to work real hard to re-create the pain, and you can't quite get there, that's when your better."
                                        Jane Fonda

Healing takes place once the wound, or cause of the problem has been found, cleansed and treated. Hypnosis can speed up this process, not only for mental and emotional healing, but also for physical healing.

Earlier in the book I explained how stress is the real culprit. Stress creates "dis-ease" which in turn, without treatment, can lead to disease. Relaxation alone can be a catalyst to the healing process since it makes the immune system stronger. Once you are able to let go of the tension and the anger, which usually surround illness of any kind, your immune system can get a boost, and you can begin the repairing or healing process.

There are probably hundreds of books about self-healing and using imagery and visualization techniques to speed the process. I'm not going to rewrite or copy any of them. What I do want to stress is that illness truly is psychosomatic (psycho meaning the mind, and soma meaning the body). This term as long been used erroneously as meaning, "it's all in the mind." The true meaning of the term, mind-body, is that the mind and the body work together. They are interdependent. It is when the mind and body are working together, when our thoughts and our energy are positive and relaxed, that miracles can happen.

Dr. Bernie Siegel, in all of his books, looks at the power of the mind in the healing process and cites case after case of healing taking place once the patient has accepted and taken control of the illness. This is what it's all about -- acceptance and taking control!

Hypnosis is extremely powerful because it can bypass our critical mind and reach that emotional subconscious much faster than through usual therapies. In fact, with medical hypnosis, direct suggestion alone works in many instances. Take warts for example. It's been proven over and over in hypnosis sessions around the world, when clients are given the suggestion that as they relax and take control of their bodies, the warts will begin to disappear, amazing things happen. When given these suggestions, along with positive affirmations and changing their energy, the warts actually begin to fall off during the session. The same success can be repeated when dealing with psoriasis, and other dermatological problems. After being given direct suggestion, many clients immediately begin the healing process with dead skin actually falling off during the session. Within 24 hours, their bodies are completely free of the rash and scales.

More dramatic "miracles" have occurred among my clients. In Europe, one of my workshop students was a young man in a wheel chair. I noticed that although he claimed he could not walk, he seemed to have no problem standing up. As I watched him, I saw that his legs were actually strong and holding him. It seemed that if he could stand somewhat comfortably, he could most likely walk, if he allowed it to happen. We spoke briefly during the breaks about the automobile accident that put him in the wheel chair, and I suggested to him that he may want to use hypnosis to assist him to walk again. A month later he returned to another workshop. He was so amazed with the changes he had begun to make in himself in one month's time, that he believed walking was possible. In fact, he allowed me to hypnotize him, after which he got off his wheel chair and walked. From then on, he used crutches -- no more chair -- and began the process of learning to walk again.

I've also had clients who were so focused that they healed themselves of cancer. These are not everyday occurrences, but with the right belief system and with determination and focus, I believe that it can become a common happening. I am in no way suggesting that we should do away with our physicians. I believe we should get all the help we can, from every avenue available. I am, however, suggesting that we take control of our own bodies.

One particular woman came to me because she was diagnosed as having liver cancer. She had a strong belief system that, as long as she stayed focused and had a purpose, she could win the battle. Her positive attitude, and her love for her granddaughter, are the keys to her wellness. During her session, I learned how much she loved her 5 year old granddaughter. I asked her to imagine herself at her granddaughter's 18th birthday party. She was able to put herself there and experience it with such reality that she described the dress she was wearing and the one her granddaughter wore. She was so happy and felt so good at this party, that I made this image her trigger. Every time she practices her self healing, she brings back that image of attending that 18th birthday celebration, knowing how very much she wants to be there. This gives her the purpose to continue keeping the positive attitude in her healing process. As of this writing her cancer is gone.

Another example of how our minds affect our health is that of a client fighting Hepatitis B. She just couldn't seem to get well. During the hypnosis session I learned she was having marital problems. She commented "If it kills me, I am going to stay married to this man." Surely this is exactly what was happening.

Our minds are extremely powerful and through hypnosis we can harness the power and use it for positive, healing change.

The bottom line is, put your two most powerful machines together -- your mind and your body -- and you are bound to be victorious.

CHAPTER 16 - THE ATHLETE'S SECRET WEAPON

Whether an amateur or professional, today's athletes are learning that mental training is as important as physical training. To be a winner, you must be able to see yourself winning. You must be able to imagine making that perfect shot, making that perfect catch, running that perfect race, making that perfect putt, etc.

I, personally, work with some wonderful athletes who are extremely focused and really understand the concept of the mind and body working together. I help them to understand that mental practice is as important as their training sessions. In fact, a study was conducted with three groups of basketball players. The first group trained in the gym every day for one month. The second group did nothing at all in the way of training. The third group practiced mentally every day for a month, giving it the same concentration and time as those in the gym.

At the end of the month, the performance of each group was measured. The first group's performance was increased by 23 percent. The second group showed no improvement at all. The surprise was the third group -- the one's who practiced mentally. Their improvement matched the first group that practiced in the gym every day. Mental practice is powerful!

In order to do their best, athletes must be focused and

relaxed. Their performance must be a natural extension of their being, not contrived in any way. It is something they do not have to think about, they just do it. The emotions of peak performance, of winning, are what keep them focused. Sometimes, however, blockages get in the way.

Karen Botha, a talented track and field star from South Africa, is a wonderful athlete. When apartheid ended and she was able to compete in the women's long jump in the 1992 Olympics in Spain, she was thrilled. She had trained hard and was very excited about the Games. However, her first qualifying jump at The Olympics was short. She still had two more tries, and she knew she was one of the top long jumpers in the world. But, when she got up there for the second jump, all she could think about was how short the previous jump had been, and again, she jumped short. Her third jump was also a failure. She had spent years of waiting and training to make it to the Olympics, and now she was not even able to compete. She was devastated. Her focus was gone.

I met Karen during my first trip to South Africa, in 1995, and began talking with her about her experience. She was back to training and competing, with a goal of competing in the 1996 Olympics in Atlanta. She was very excited and very focused, but she was afraid of repeating the failure in the qualifying rounds. As I worked with Karen, I explained that we had to change her focus when she was about to make her jump. She knew her routine, she knew the physical routine of preparation for a jump. Her body knew exactly how to move and how to jump in order to win. It was second nature to her. She really didn't even have to think about it, she just had to do it. That *fear* of the short jump, however, stood in her way.

I had Karen relax, and focus on her favorite number, the number 10. As she would begin her routine, which she could do in her sleep, all she had to focus on was that number 10. By focusing on this number 10, she would be relaxed, nothing could disturb her, and she would make her perfect jump. During the session I made a reinforcement tape for her and had her listen to it at least once every day. When she completed the session, she felt wonderful and extremely positive.

It just so happened that the following week-end, while I was conducting another seminar, Karen was competing in an international track and field event, which was being televised on South Africa's version of Wide World of Sports. I knew the time of the competition, and asked that a television set be rolled into the classroom. We all watched as, during the qualification jumps, Karen broke a world record in the women's long jump!

Karen's husband, Naas Botha, is a world famous rugby player. Naas even played for the Dallas Cowboys for a season, but returned to his homeland when he was unable to attain the stardom in the States that he has in South Africa and Europe. Naas is the best there is in rugby, but what he wanted to do was to improve his golf game. As a competitive athlete, he is always pushing himself to be the very best at every sport he plays. His problem with golf was that he just did not attack the game and play it with the fervor he had for rugby. He needed focus. In my session with Naas, we worked on his focus and mental imagery of the game of golf. He would mentally practice, playing the game in his head, hole by hole. Seeing each play on the course, and seeing himself making the perfect drive or putt. I also left Naas with a reinforcement audiotape which he listened to every day. Naas' game was so improved in a few months, it was as if he had become a professional golfer.

I also work with a professional boxer, Daren Zenner. Daren is extremely creative, and has an incredible amount of focus. He came to me first as a student of hypnotherapy, and then as a client. Now, I work with him before each fight. We treat each fight individually. At first, I worked with him to imagine the fighter he admired most. He had to see the moves that fighter made which he could use. I didn't have him imagine himself being that fighter, or fighting like that fighter. I had him instead take the great moves of that fighter, and make them his. It had to be him fighting, using his own abilities. Through hypnosis, he has really developed his mental and physical fighting techniques. Now, as each fight comes up, we look at his opponent, how that opponent fights, where his strengths and weaknesses are. By the time Daren gets into the ring for the real fight, he has already won it hundreds of times in his mind! His goal is to hold the World Super-Middleweight Title. I believe he will!

At the end of 1994, I was invited to Japan to do a 1995 New Year's Special called "Make Your Dreams Come True." Hypnotists from around the world were invited to work with some of Japan's celebrities. I was given the assignment to work with two movie stars who are Japan's version of Doris Day and Cary Grant. They wanted to improve their golf game. I met them on the golf course at a country club outside of Tokyo, and along with the club's golf pro, I watched them play a few holes (very badly, I might add.) The pro explained to me what they were doing wrong, and how they could improve. I then took them into the clubhouse and hypnotized the two of them together.

Being actors, pretending was easy for them. Their imaginations were well developed, and it was easy for them to understand imagery I gave them for their focus. After the hypnosis we returned to the course. The results were outstanding! Their driving was straight and well placed, and their putts were accurate. This was all shown on Japan's NTV's 1995 New Year's Day Special. It was absolutely amazing.

I've worked with bowlers and baseball players as well, and the mental game is the key. Each athlete must be able to see, hear and feel the win mentally, before it can actually happen. In order to play that super game, or make that super performance, the athlete must be able to perform without thinking about it. The mind and the body must work together, both knowing their jobs, without effort and without "trying." Problems arise when a bad experience, at a certain spot or during a certain movement, cause bad performance, such as a missed step, a bad swing, etc. The emotions surrounding that bad performance, like Karen's failure to make the jump for instance, are triggered at that particular moment of the jump, at that particular hole on the golf course, or at a specific bowling alley. To regain control the athlete must let go of that memory. The athlete must release it so that the trigger will not elicit that negative response.

Each and every athlete, amateur, professional, or backyard, can improve his or her performance by practicing mentally. Self-hypnosis is a special passport to athletic success.

CHAPTER 17 - TECHNIQUES THAT WORK

I've talked a lot about becoming a winner, and have given you examples of how hypnosis and self-hypnosis can help you towards that goal. Now I'd like to give you some techniques you can use immediately to put you on your own road to success.

Develop your Photographic Memory

Our brains are wonderful organs. Stored in them is everything we have ever heard, seen or read. Everything! Why is it, then, that we just cannot seem to remember at will? The main reason is that we are *trying* too hard. It's back to that word "try!" We try so hard to remember or recall something, that it just doesn't surface.

How many times have you been talking on the phone or with someone, and they asked you for the name of a person or a restaurant, and you *tried and tried* to remember and it just would not come to you. However, as soon as you hung up, or the person left, that name came right back. It was there, stored in your mind, but just would not surface because you were "trying too hard." As soon as you stopped trying and let it go, there it was!

Here's a simple technique to make the recalling process much easier, and much less frustrating. From now on, when you can't remember something, instead of focusing on it

84

and "trying" to remember, merely say to yourself, "In a moment, I'll remember." Just repeat, to yourself, "In a moment, I'll remember." Then, just forget about it. Let it go. You'll find that in a few moments, what you were *trying* to remember will just pop right up in your mind.

I've taught this technique to thousands of my students because it's so simple and it works!

Develop your Success/Prosperity Consciousness

A simple exercise performed each day will put you on the road to success and prosperity. Earlier I spoke about getting back what you put out. In order to reap the bounty that the universe has to offer, all you must really do is let the universe know what it is you want or need. Whether you are seeking that perfect relationship, a new and more rewarding job, success and abundance for your own business (or anything your mind can create), you must make your desires known.

In addition, your subconscious (that 10 year old emotional mind) must also be in agreement with your conscious mind. Therefore, you must combine your request to the universe with the programming of your subconscious. This can be done by taking 7 minutes a day to focus on just what it is you are seeking, using a form of self-hypnosis.

To begin this exercise, the first thing you will need is a

timer with an alarm. When you sit down to focus on what it is you want, set the timer for 7 minutes and begin. Get a clear picture in your mind of yourself having attained what it is you want. For instance, if you are looking for a perfect relationship, get a clear picture of yourself having that relationship and then add to it all the emotions and feelings of having that relationship. If its prosperity you are seeking, get a clear picture of yourself having the money to do everything that would make you happy (see the home you desire, wearing the clothes you would wear, traveling) and add to that picture, all the emotions and feelings this success. In other words, for 7 minutes, until that timer rings, see, feel, hear and experience in your mind what it is like to have succeeded. Through this imagery, this pretending, you are sending out your message to the universe, as well as programming your subconscious mind. With your subconscious acting in partnership with your conscious mind, success is guaranteed.

Continue to do this exercise for 7 minutes each day and, at the end of one year, take stock in the changes in your life. Not only will you be closer to where you want to be (if you haven't already made it), but you will have developed a life-long habit of programming through self-hypnosis to help you achieve all of your dreams.

Change your thoughts to guarantee positive results

Another simple method to ensure positive programming comes from changing your negative thoughts to positive ones. Although the concept is simple, in the beginning you may find the process challenging.

Each and every time you catch yourself thinking or speaking in the negative, immediately change the statement or thought to a positive one. For example, you are driving to work, it's raining, and traffic is backed up. You think "What a miserable day to be stuck in traffic." Immediately, upon recognizing this negative thought, change the thought pattern to something like, " It's a good day to remain calm and thoughtful about my driving." Or, "Because traffic is moving slowly in the rain, I have more time to organize my day in my mind so that it runs smoothly." By taking the negatives and making something positive from them, you'll find that your entire attitude will change, and it will make a difference in how you interact to others and how they react to you. It is a challenge to catch all of the negatives and change them, but you will find that as you continue to practice this thought pattern change, it will become easier and easier, until you have a permanent positive mind set.

CHAPTER 18 - MAKE YOUR OWN PROGRAMMING TAPE

Up to this point, I have given you some easy techniques for affirmations, self-hypnosis and developing a positive consciousness. Each of these alone can be a tool in itself to put you on the winning path. Use them all, and you've boosted your success rate a hundred fold. However, add one more technique, and you are GUARANTEED success!

The final technique, is making yourself your own self-programming audio tapes. If you've been in any of the New Age Stores, or the "self help" tape section of many of the larger book store chains, you have seen audio and subliminal tapes to lose weight, stop smoking, increase your breast size, make more sales, have more self-confidence -- I can go on and on. If you sit in front of your television set and channel surf, you will come across a wide variety of infomercials all selling you a book and/or tape set to program yourself or to motivate you. These all cost a pretty penny because someone else has taken the initiative to write the scripts and make the recording, have them duplicated, marketed and then distributed. These are all helpful -- if you use them properly. But, keep in mind that these books and tapes are all very general to the topic, because they must take into account all of the different people that are buying them.

If you really want to use audio tapes for self-programming,

the best way to go is to make your own, First of all, by making your own tapes, they are very personal, and deal with your personal blocks, personal goals and objectives, and, most important, your belief system. And second, your subconscious actually responds better to your own voice, than to the voice of another. You may not think you like your voice on tape, but your subconscious likes it best of all.

Here are your step-by-step instructions for making your own programming tapes.

<u>Equipment</u>

Fancy equipment is not necessary. A blank audio cassette tape and a simple cassette recorder are all that are you really need to get started. Although, if you wish to make more professional tapes for yourself, you might invest in a karaoke machine and some meditation music cassettes, which will allow you to put music to your voice recording. Remember, the important thing is, once you make the tape, you must listen to it regularly -- once a day for at least 21 days -- in order for that programming to really work.

I, personally, like to listen to my tapes at bedtime. I put them on after I'm in bed, and usually fall asleep. This is fine, because in the early stages of sleep, the subconscious mind still gets the message. Because this is my preferred listening time, I have a cassette deck that turns off automatically at the end of the tape.

Remember, the more simple you make it, the better the chance that you will succeed.

Beginning your Recording

Each recording should start with some guided imagery for relaxation. You can write your own technique and read it, or you can take some examples from the scripts in the appendix. The important part of this step is to assist you to relax your body and your mind.

Some people respond to the relaxation in two or three minutes; the average person needs about six or seven minutes of relaxation; and there are some who need as much as ten or twelve minutes. I suggest you prepare a six or seven minute guided relaxation script. Record it by reading it slowly. Then, listen to it and see how you feel. If by the end of the relaxation you feel nice and relaxed, then it's long enough. If you've actually fallen asleep, it may be too long, and if you're still squirming around, it may be too short.

The Convincer

It is important for you to be "convinced" that you are actually hypnotized. When you work with a hypnotherapist, a convincer is always used. For example, he may suggest that when he raises your arm, it will become stiff and rigid, like a bar of steel, and no matter how hard you try, you cannot lower the arm. Or, he may suggest that your eye lids are stuck together stuck like glue, and no matter how hard you try to open them, you will be unable to do so. These little "tests" <u>convince</u> the conscious mind that you are indeed hypnotized. The same thing holds true when you are making a tape for yourself.

Here is a simple convincer for you to use in your own tape, after the relaxation and before the programming:

> *"Now that you are relaxed, I'd like you to focus your attention on the muscles around your eyes. Just focus on the muscles around your eyes and allow those muscles to relax completely. Just allow the muscles around your eyes to relax so completely, that your eyes will not open. In fact, when you are certain that those muscles are so relaxed that your eyes will not open, just test them. When you are absolutely certain that your eyes will not open, try to open them, but you cannot. Just try to open them. but you cannot. Good.......very good.":*

This simple "convincer" allows your conscious mind to understand that you are indeed relaxed and ready for programming.

The Programming

Once you are relaxed, and you have done the convincer, you are ready to begin the programming. Whether this programing is to let go of unwanted weight, to play a better golf game, to find the perfect relationship, or to build success in your job or business, it is imperative to follow the six points of programming

1.   Speak in the Second Person

When you are making the tape, you are talking to yourself, but you are talking to the subconscious part of yourself and therefore call yourself "You." Unlike self-hypnosis and affirmation techniques, which are done in the first person ("I am healthy. I am prosperous." etc.) programming with audio tapes is done in the second person.

2.   Be Positive

As I explained earlier, the subconscious mind does not understand negatives. When you say "I will not..." to the subconscious, it hears "I will." You must, therefore, make certain that your programming is done with very positive statements.

For instance, if you wish to stop smoking, instead of saying "You do not smoke," say "You are smoke free." If you are programming to let go of weight, instead of saying "You do not eat fried foods," say "You eat only low fat and healthy foods." Get the idea?

If you find there is no way around a negative, the only way the subconscious mind will get it is to repeat it: "You do not, I repeat, not........." In the case of the negative, you must always say the "not, I repeat, not" in that way for the subconscious to grasp it.

I have a simple example of how this works. All of you who have or are around small children from time to time will appreciate this. When you say to a child "Do not put your feet on the couch/run in the house/touch the stove," etc., what is the first thing that child does? Right! Exactly what you just told him or her NOT TO DO! Next time you find yourself telling a child NOT to do something, use the "I repeat not" technique. "Do not, I repeat, not, put your feet on the couch!" You will be amazed at the results.

3.   Use the Present Tense

The subconscious mind accepts only the present. There is no conception of what will or might happen, only what is. Therefore, as you write your program, you must see it as already existing. You are doing it NOW. Not yesterday, not tomorrow, not next week. It is NOW! Instead of saying "I will eat better" (this is positive), say "I eat better" (this is positive, and in the now, in the present).

4.   <u>Be Specific</u>

This point, gets to the point. YOU GOTTA HAVE A PLAN! You can visualize, you can affirm, you can meditate until the cows come home, but unless you have a plan you are going nowhere.

Some good examples include your desire to let go of those 25 extra pounds. You know that unless you change your eating habits and add exercise to your life, it's not going to happen. Now, what's your plan. Okay, your programming includes "I eat only low fat, healthy foods." That's fine it's specific -- low fat, healthy. The subconscious understands that reading the label can determine the fat content, and healthy includes fruits and vegetables, little to no red meat. You can get more specific if you wish to eliminate certain foods such as red meat, sugar and white flour. These are personal tastes. Be as specific as possible. However, let's talk about the exercise. Here you say "I will work out every Monday, Wednesday and Friday." NO - - Not specific. Okay, "I will work out

every Monday, Wednesday and Friday afternoon."
NO -- Not specific. Okay. "I will work out every
Monday, Wednesday and Friday at 3:00 PM." AHA!
Now you've got it!

The main thing you must do for this step is to make
your plan, and then write it into your program.
Without a specific plan, you don't know what you'll
get. A hypnotherapist I know, who had just ended a
bad marriage, wanted to program herself for a
relationship. After talking with me, she said, "I'll do
it myself, I know how, I'm a hypnotherapist. I know
what must be done.." So, she set about writing her
program and affirmations, and making a tape. She
focused on "I want a man who is rich. I want a man
who is rich. I want a man who is rich." Two years
later I met her at a convention and asked her if she
found her relationship. She looked at me and said,
"Well, I found a relationship, but I'm now in the
process of another divorce." I asked her what
happened. She said, "Well, I kept asking for a man
who is rich, and guess what. The man I married was
named Rich!" It was truly a case of "Be careful
what you ask for, because you will probably get it."
She was not specific about what "rich" meant. I
implore you, be very specific!

5. Be Believable/Realistic/Repetitive

It is absolutely necessary that what you are planning to do must be realistic. As an adult, if you are doing a tape to become 5 inches taller, this is not realistic (unless you are going for bone implant surgery). However, if you wish to focus on your posture to "stand taller," this is realistic. If you say you will work-out 7 days a week, this is usually unrealistic, while 2 to 3 days a week is realistic. Remember, you are setting yourself up for success, not failure. By being realistic, you will be successful. Make certain you are being realistic and that you believe you can do it or achieve it the way you are programming it. Then repeat it over and over. The more times you repeat your programming, the better you will do. Find different ways to say the same thing, just so that suggestion gets from your conscious to your subconscious, making your subconscious your partner in success.

6. The Programming Must Carry A Reward

Everyone likes to be rewarded, and the subconscious and the conscious minds are no different. Your programming must carry with it a reward of some kind. For instance, the reward of letting go of weight, could be "wearing that size 10 dress." The reward for success at the job could mean "obtaining that bonus." Always, but always, make certain there is a reward connected with your program.

Closing and Wake-Up

To close your tape you have three choices:

1. Wake yourself.

    When and where you plan on listening to your programming tape can dictate the closing. If you plan to listen to it during the day, first thing in the morning, or perhaps early evening, then you'll want to program yourself for waking and feeling energetic and wonderful.

    The verbiage for such a wake up should be as follows:

    "In a moment I'm going to count from 1 to 5, and at the count of five you will wake up feeling better than you've felt in a long time. You will awaken feeling wonderful and full of energy. 1------coming up; 2---------feeling wonderful; 3-----------feeling better than you've felt in a long time; 4------------waking up; 5-------------eyes open, feeling terrific!"

2. <u>Suggest A Wonderful Night's Sleep</u>

If you plan to listen to the programming tape at night when you go to bed, then perhaps you will want to program yourself for a wonderful night's sleep, waking in the morning feeling energetic and wonderful: The verbiage for this could read:

"Now as you allow these wonderful thoughts, this wonderful programming, these wonderful affirmations to go round and round in your mind, you drift off into a wonderfully sound sleep. You drift into a wonderful, sound, restful sleep. And when you wake at your usual time (give a specific time, if you wish), you will awaken feeling fully rested, full of energy and feeling terrific. You drift into a wonderful, sound, restful sleep, waking at your usual time feeing fully rested, full of energy and feeling terrific."

3. <u>Give Yourself A Choice</u>

If you are not certain which time will be best for you -- during the day or before bed -- you can actually give yourself the choice, depending on when you listen to the tape on any particular day. Here's a sample:

"As this wonderful programming continues to echo throughout your mind, and if this is your bedtime, you allow yourself to drift into a wonderful, sound and restful sleep now. If this is your bedtime, just allow yourself now to drift into a wonderful, sound and restful sleep and you will awaken in the morning, fully rested, full of positive energy and feeling terrific. However, if you wish to awaken, I will now count from 1 to 5, and at the count of five you will awaken, feeing wonderful and full of positive energy. 1......coming up; 2.........feeling better than you've felt in a long time; 3------------full of positive thoughts and energy; 4-------beginning to awaken; and 5-------eyes open, feeling wonderful!"

Now Just Do It!

There. You have the magic formula for audio tape programming and your guarantee to win. Now it's up to you! Follow the easy steps I've given you and just do it!

APPENDIX

Following are three complete scripts ready for recording for your own use. When recording you should remember:

1.   Read slowly and take your time. There is no rush.

2.   The more monotonous your tone of voice, the better.

3.   Your subconsious mind reacts better to your own voice than another's voice.

4.   You may mix and match guided relaxation and waking with any programming script you write for yourself.

FINDING YOUR INNER CHILD SCRIPT

What I would like you to do now, is to sit back, or lie back; just get comfortable. And when you are comfortable, I'd like you to take a deep breath...and exhale. Now just close down your eyes, and take another deep breath...hold it...and exhale slowly...and as you exhale, just allow your entire body to relax and let go. Good, very good.

I'd like you to focus your attention on all the muscles around your eyes. Just focus all your attention on the tiny muscles around your eyes, and as you do, just allow those muscles to relax completely. Allow them to relax so completely that your eyes will not be able to open. Now, allow those muscles to relax, so that your eyes will not be able to open...and, when you're sure that these muscles are so relaxed that your eyes will not open...when you are absolutely certain, that your eyes will not open, just give them a test...just try to open them, and you will see you cannot. Just test them, and see that they will not open. Good, very good.

I'd like you to take one more deep breath...hold it...and slowly begin to exhale. And as you exhale, just allow the relaxation around your eyes, to go all the way down to the tips of your toes.

Now, I'd like you to focus your attention on your toes, and just allow your toes to completely relax. Just let go, and allow the toes to relax completely. Then, allow that relaxation to move upward, relaxing your feet...relaxing your ankles...relaxing your calves...just letting go. And that relaxation continues upward, relaxing your knees...your thighs...your hips. Good... Now, continuing upward, your abdomen and lower back relax....your waist and middle back relax and let go...your chest and upper back relax...feeling so good. Now, your shoulders relax, and the relaxation moves down your arms...upper arms...elbows...lower arms...wrists...hands....all the way down to the tips of your fingers. Warm, soothing relaxation. Now, your neck relaxes...your jaw and all the muscles around your mouth relax, and as they relax, your jaw drops slightly, totally relaxed. Your cheeks relax, your nose...your ears...your eyes...your forehead relaxes...even your scalp relaxes. Feeling so good...so relaxed....just letting go...Good...very good.

I'd like you now to imagine yourself at the top of a staircase...a staircase with ten steps in all...and these steps are covered in your favorite color of carpet...and as you look down, you notice how beautiful this staircase is. I'm going to count from ten down to one, and with each number that I count, I want you to take a step down the staircase....with each number that I count, and each step that you take, you will become more and more relaxed...with each step you will allow your relaxation to double. So that when you get to the bottom, you will be in a very, very deep state of relaxation...And, when you get to the bottom, there will be someone there to meet you....a small child will be there to meet you...this will be your Inner Child.

Okay, here we go.

10- Take the first step down, just allowing the relaxation you are feeling to double.

9- Take the second step down, growing more and more relaxed

8- Doubling again the relaxation you are feeling

7- Deeper and deeper

6- Always feeling comfortable, but allowing yourself to go deeper into relaxation

5- Halfway down, continuing to listen to my voice

4- Feeling wonderful, so very relaxed and going deeper

3- Nearing the bottom, more sleepy, more drowsy, more relaxed

2- Almost there, and beginning to approach that child waiting for you

1- At the bottom, very, very deeply relaxed, and walking up to the child waiting for you...

As you approach that lovely, wonderful child waiting for you, notice who this child really is. This child is your Inner Child -- that part of you that remains innocent, vulnerable, yet curious and hopeful. Now reach down, pick up that child, your Inner Child, and hold that child in your arms. Allow that child to experience, to feel the love you have for (him or her). And, as you hold that child, talk to that child, addressing (him or her) by your first name. Say, (your first name), I know that you feel guilty about many things, about many hurts that you've had in your life, but I want you to know that I forgive you. I forgive you and I want you to know that I love you. I will always love you, I will always take care of you, and I will always protect you. I will never let any harm come to you, for you are my precious Inner Child.

Continue holding your Inner Child, and experience that wonderful unconditional love, between you and the child within. Allow unconditional love to pour in both directions, to and from this child. Hold this child...love this child...for this child is you...that inner, childlike part of you that always needs your love.

Now allow that Inner Child to be absorbed into your being. And as that child is absorbed into your being, notice the love and the comfort beginning to permeate within you. To fill and surround you. You have found your Inner Child, and that child will always be with you.

In a moment, I'm going to count from one to five. When I reach the number five, you will open your eyes, feeling wonderful, feeling loved, feeling better than you've felt in a long time. Feeling whole.

1-   Coming up
2-   Beginning to feel more alive than you've felt in a

long time

3- Starting to stretch out
4- Noticing how much you want to smile
5- Eyes open, feeling wonderful, feeling loved, feeling whole....

STRESS REDUCTION SCRIPT

This is a program for deep relaxation. You will experience a growing sense of calm in both your mind and your body. You will feel yourself relaxing more and more fully. When you are finished you will feel refreshed. The instructions I will give you are easy. You will have no trouble following them. So hear my voice and let your mind and body respond naturally without effort. Use my voice as a guide for your feelings and sensations. You are about to participate in an interactive experience. I will ask you to participate by using your vivid imagination in a very active way to help achieve the results that you desire.

Now close your eyes and relax. Just for a moment imagine all the muscle groups in your body letting go. Take a deep breath. That's good. Exhale now, and take another deep breath and exhale. Each time that you breathe from here on, imagine your breath flowing out through your rib cage and spreading relaxation throughout your body. Feel that relaxation as I talk to you. Relax all the muscle groups around your face for a moment. Relax your scalp, your forehead, your eyebrows, your eyelids, and relax your cheeks and your nose and your mouth and especially those muscle groups around your mouth and lips. If your teeth are clenched together, unclench them and you will relax even more.

The first step in relaxation is to relax your chin and jaw.

Now just relax. Relax your chin and jaw, and allow all those muscles in your face to just let go. And now your neck muscles relax, the front part of your neck and the back part of your neck, right through to your shoulders. Feel your shoulders relaxing completely. Get rid of any tension that might be in your shoulder area. It feels so good to do that. And allow your arms to relax. Your upper arms relax, your elbows, your forearms relax. Relax your wrists, your hands, even your fingers relax and let go. Just imagine for a moment that your arms are becoming very heavy, loose and limp, heavy, loose and limp like a wet wash cloth.

And now allow yourself to breathe comfortably, and pay attention to your breathing. Notice how much more deep and regular your breathing has become than just a few moments ago when we started. Feel your breathing. Feel the rhythm of your breathing. Notice the contraction and expansion of your diaphragm and your chest. Allow your chest muscles to relax completely, right down through to your stomach area. Feel your stomach muscles just relaxing. Get rid of any tension that might be in that area, and allow your back muscles to relax now, those large muscle groups in the upper part of your back, right down your spinal column to your lower back. Just let go, let go completely, and allow those smaller muscle groups in the lower part of your back to relax as well.

Relax your hips, and especially your legs. Allow your thighs to relax now, your knees, your calves, your ankles,

108

your feet, and even your toes. Just allow those muscle groups to just relax completely as you begin to drift into a very deep relaxed state, letting yourself go, letting your mind and body become one, feeling good, feeling so good now. Many people sitting there as you are now report certain feelings in their body. Some people report a numbness in their arms or legs. Some people report a tingling feeling such as pins and needles, usually in their hands or arms, or some report both a numbness and tingling feeling alternately. Some people experience a lightness in their body, and others experience a heaviness. If you experience a lightness, it would seem as though you were feeling buoyant, as though you were floating above the chair. If you experience a heaviness, it would feel as though you were sinking into the chair shoulders sagging.

And some people, when they relax find they have a need to swallow because their salivary glands dry up. So if you have a need to swallow it's perfectly okay to do so. Many people also find that when they let go and relax their eyeballs relax in their socket and their eyelids begin to flicker or flutter ever so lightly. This is an excellent sign of letting go. Some people even report experiencing some sort of sensory distortion or detachment in their body. Their arms may be where their legs are or vice versa. This too is a good sign of letting go and relaxing. The important thing with these signs is that if you experienced any of these signs at all, it indicates your willingness and readiness to allow yourself to go into a very deep and relaxed hypnotic rest.

And going into hypnosis is very gradual, so gradual indeed that in a moment I'm going to count down from twenty to one. On each count you can allow yourself to drift into hypnosis at your own pace. But before I do that just imagine a custom-made cloud snuggling up to your body in the shape of a chair, and imagine this chair has arms on it. It is a very warm and comfortable cloud. It is your personal cloud. Notice how it snuggles up to your body, and now it is going to take you to a very beautiful place, a special place in your life, a very comfortable place, a place where you're happy, a place where you feel good, a place where you look good. So allow this custom cloud now to just snuggle up to your body and to just take you to your special place where you're happy, relaxed and very calm. Allow yourself to be there for a moment as I begin to count and you go deeper and deeper into hypnosis.

Twenty -- going deeper and deeper now. Nineteen.....all the way down deep. Eighteen...deeper, Seventeen...tired and drowsy... Sixteen .....deeper. Fifteen....just letting go .... Fourteen ......deeper. Thirteen ....deeper and deeper...... Twelve...... deeper...Eleven...... all the way down deep......Ten....deeper and deeper.....Nine.....just letting go....... Eight....deeper and deeper..... Seven......going deeper. Six....... deeper. Five ..... deeper and deeper......Four.... still deeper......Three... all the way down......Two.....and Finally, One......deep, deep, deep hypnosis. Your mind is very relaxed and open to receive the helpful and beneficial suggestions I'm about to give you.

I'd like you to focus on the number seven. See the number seven with a background behind the number. See the number seven. And, as you look at that number seven, I'd like you to know that all the stress, all the tension, all the anxiety, all the strains, all the bad feelings leave your body now. As you focus on that number on that number seven, as you focus on that number seven and watch it as it begins to fade away. As you watch it fade away, all the stress, all the tension, all the anxiety, all the strains, all the bad feelings leave your body, and as the number seven is now replaced by the number six, that number six tells you it is working. And all the stress, all the tension, all the anxiety, all the strains, all the bad feelings have left your body and you feel good, you feel wonderful and you feel fine.

You find yourself now with more energy than you have had for a long, long time. And you find that by thinking positive thoughts, and functioning with positive energy and positive emotions, things in your life start happening now, things in your life start opening up now, things in your life start becoming very clear now. And every day, you have more and more confidence in your ability, more and more confidence concerning who you are. And, your self-esteem is now so strong that you find now you are able to focus and accomplish things that you have been meaning to do. Every day you feel more and more internally aligned, able to experience life directly, fully in touch with your own feelings.

I'd also like you to know that any time in the future you would like to feel as relaxed as you are, only more so, all you have to do is take a deep breath, count one, two, three, just touch your thumb together with your forefinger and you will begin to drift into a wonderful state of relaxation where you are able to give yourself suggestions to improve your own life.

Now relax and rest, and in a moment I'll count from one to five. At the count of five you'll open your eyes. You'll be wide awake and alert, and all the helpful and beneficial suggestions given to you will go deep into the unconscious part of your mind where they do the most good. You'll be able to recall them whenever you need to. One, starting to emerge from hypnosis now, coming all the way back. Two, becoming more and more alert. Three, your mind is becoming clear and alert. Four, remembering everything told to you. And five, eyes open when you're ready, feeling fine in every way. Five, eyes open, feeling wonderful.

PAST-LIFE REGRESSION SCRIPT

Sit back, or lie back, and make yourself very comfortable. Close your eyes and take a deep breath and exhale. Take another deep breath ----- and exhale -- letting go, relaxing your body. And, take yet another deep breath ---- and exhale, relaxing your body, feeling your mind beginning to relax also. Now take one more deep breath --- and exhale --- relax your body, relax your mind --- just let go and listen to my voice.

Just imagine a beautiful white light over your head. Now imagine this white light entering the top of your head and moving down, bringing a wonderful feeling of relaxation as it flows through your body. Feel your head relax as the muscles in your forehead begin to let go. This relaxation flows through your facial muscles around your eyes, your cheeks, your mouth. All the facial muscles relaxing. As your mouth relaxes, your jaw also relaxes, unclenching your teeth. Deeper and deeper relaxed. Very good.

Now the relaxation moves down to the neck muscles, letting go, relaxing. The shoulders relax, all tension disappearing, and this wave of relaxation moves down through your arms, into your hands and fingers -- relaxing more, Deeper and deeper relaxed.

Your back muscles begin to let go, relaxing, deeper and deeper, as this wave of relaxation moves down through your hips and into your thighs, your knees, your ankles and down into your feet. Your whole body now deeply, so deeply relaxed.

Now I'd like you to imagine a staircase, a staircase with ten steps in all and the stairs are covered with your favorite color carpet. I will count from 10 down to 1 and with each number that I count you will take a step down, and with each step down, you will become more comfortable, more relaxed. With each step you will go deeper and deeper into relaxation.

10	take the first step, feeling more and more relaxed
9	take the second step, a hundred times deeper
8	down deeper, feeling yourself growing more relaxed
7	Feeling the relaxation flowing through your body
6	Relaxing more and more with each step that you take
5	A thousand times deeper, feeling very calm and relaxed
4	Relaxation flowing through every nerve, muscle and tendon of your body
3	Almost at the bottom of the staircase, very calm, very peaceful
2	Becoming very deeply relaxed; and,.
1	Deeply relaxed. Peaceful and ready for this wonderful journey..

Now I'd like you to focus on the top of your head. Focus on the top of your head and see a door. Now see the door open, and as this door on the top of your head opens, you allow yourself to float out of your body which is so comfortable, so safe, so relaxed. You float out and feel an incredible freedom. The freedom to move effortlessly in space and time. So free, so safe, so relaxed. And as you begin to accustom yourself to this freedom of movement, you allow yourself to float up higher and higher. Up over the houses and buildings of your community, looking down. Look down at your very own house or apartment building, see your neighborhood. Study it. It's all very familiar. Can you see it? Can you see your neighborhood? Nod your head. Good -- very good. Allow yourself to float over your neighborhood for a bit -- see it, see your neighbors going about their business. Enjoy the experience of looking around as you float above all the hustle and bustle of everyday life. You are so relaxed, so free, just floating in space and time.

Now as you look around you, you see some beautiful white clouds, beautiful white, fluffy clouds. These clouds look so inviting, and you notice a tunnel through the clouds. How wonderful - a lovely tunnel which goes right through the clouds and you know that on the other side of the tunnel, through the beautiful white clouds, is another time, another place where you have been before in a previous life. Another time, another place, and you can go there because you are able to move so easily and effortlessly through time and space.

And as I count from 5 to 1, you will enter the tunnel and when I reach the number 1 you will be in another body, in another time and another place - in a previous life -- a life you experienced before this one, a life from which you can learn something about your present life.

5 Entering the tunnel, so peaceful, calm and relaxed
4 Moving through the tunnel, easily, effortlessly
3 Continuing on, back in time and space
2 In a moment you will be on the other side, in another body in a previous lifetime -- going back in time and space.
1 Through the tunnel, in a previous body, in a previous lifetime

Now, as you accustomed yourself to this different, but familiar, body take a moment and look around. Look around at the scenery, breath the air, smell the scents and odors, feel the ground beneath your feet. Where are you? Inside or outside? Look around. It's all familiar, you just have not been here in a very, very long time. Now look down at your feet. Are you wearing shoes? If you are, what do they look like? Now scan yourself. What clothes are you wearing? What do they look like? What colors? Are you a man or a woman? How old are you? What are you doing? Look around -- is there anyone with you? Is there anyone there you recognize from your present lifetime?

Go to where you live. Look around. Who is there? A meal has been prepared. What are you eating? Listen to the conversation at the table. What is going on? What is your family like? How do you fit into this family? Are you the mother? The father? The child? Notice all your family members and how you relate to them.

Now take some time and explore this lifetime. There is something in this lifetime that affects your present lifetime. Just listen to the music and allow yourself to explore and learn.

Now it's time to experience yourself getting older and actually moving on to your death in this previous life, and as you move to the death scene of this previous life you actually float back out of this body from this past time and past place so that you can see the death scene from above. Just look down and see what is happening -- without fear, without pain, just observing and gaining understanding. Observe and understand.

Now allow yourself to experience your life between lives. Feel your total connection to the loving "Source" energy, your one-ness with all.

And now, as you float in time and space you again see the tunnel in the clouds. And as I count from 1 to 5 you go back through the clouds to the present time, to the here and now. So, approach the tunnel - safe and comfortable.

1   Moving forward in time and space
2   Effortlessly floating through the tunnel
3   Halfway back to the present
4   Almost at the end
5   Through the tunnel, floating into the present time, the
    here and now.

Now just continue floating easily and effortlessly, seeing
below you the familiar sights and hearing the sounds of
your neighborhood, yet remembering the past life you have
just re-experienced. You feel so good, having remembered
and having learned a valuable lesson for this present life.
And as you reflect upon this adventure you see your present
body, the body in the here and now below you and you float
back in, feeling so relaxed, so safe, so comfortable. You are
now back in your present body, in the here and now,
relaxed, safe and comfortable. You have closed the door on
the top of your head, and are now totally back in the
present, totally back in the here and now. Just relax, just
relax.

In a moment I'm going to awaken you by counting from 1
to 3. When you awaken, you will feel wonderful, relaxed
and happy. In fact you will be more relaxed and happier
than you have been in a long time. You have just been on
a wonderful adventure and learned so many things and
gained more understanding about yourself. You had an
incredible time and feel so good about yourself. So now,

1   Beginning to awake,
2   Coming up feeling wonderful, happy, relaxed
3   Wide awake feeling relaxed and full of energy, with
     a new understanding of yourself.

You've had a marvelous journey and can use all of the
information you received to make your present life more
satisfying, more enjoyable and more successful.